JN090741

多文化コミュニケーション:

心が伝わる 英語の話し方

Heart to Heart English

しゅわぶ美智子

IBC

装 幀：久保頼三郎

Preface

Crossing international borders to study, work or live is anything but simple. There are nearly always more challenges, contingencies, and differences than initially imagined. Michiko Hamada Schwab comes by her border-crossing experiences, replete with concrete examples and compelling stories, quite naturally, as one will quickly ascertain on opening this book and reading almost any page. Her insights on acquiring English amount to practical wisdom that virtually all border-crossing readers, whatever their native language, could appreciate and realize in their own lives.

There may well be particular challenges for Japanese learning foreign languages, given the twists and turns of Japanese history and culture, but challenges also confront those wanting to learn Japanese. Located off the Asian mainland, Japan stands apart geographically and, in its isolation—compounded by nearly two-and-a-half centuries of officially closed borders (1630s–1860s)—has often appeared to the outside world, even now, as self-absorbed, even closed off, and that has contributed to making the socio-linguistic transition for Japanese leaving Japan and foreigners arriving there somewhat discombobulating at best, intensely stressful, even painful, at worst.

That transition can certainly constitute a substantial roadblock to effectively adapting to the new culture. Studying a taxonomy of world languages, one notices that English has close connections with Sanskrit, the Romance and Germanic languages, while Japanese is alone on a limb, unconnected with any other language (though it shares a few grammatical properties with Korean). So, when studying Japanese, non-Japanese have few analogies with a known language to help them along and no cognates at all. That kind of dilemma has resulted in a proverb-like dictum: "The earlier you begin studying Japanese, the longer it takes to learn it." Japanese surely sense something similar in their longstanding attempts to acquire English (or other Western languages).

Perhaps that dilemma confronts any adult attempting to acquire another language: all languages are full of potential cultural pitfalls. For example, I asked a Japanese expatriate, whom I was coaching and who had been in the U.S. only two months, what had been the strangest interaction he had encountered so far. "Why," he responded, "do Americans say, 'I don't know?'" So I asked him, "What's wrong with that?" He answered, "But isn't it rude?" Of course, in America, when you don't know the answer to a question, "I don't know" is considered polite, to the point, and quick (very important in the U.S., where the proverb "time is money" was created). How, I asked, would he respond to that question in Japanese? To demonstrate, he held his right elbow in his left hand, his chin in his right. He then made a thinking noise, "Hmmm," as if deeply thinking about it and, after a few seconds, said, "Um, I'm not sure." While that kind of response is considered polite in Japan, many Americans might feel that he was wasting their time. "Do you know or not? Just say it!" they might think. This example reveals how language usage is often wrapped in culture, a communication aspect inadequately covered in many language textbooks. The Japanese expat understood the words and grammatical points and his English was quite sufficient for most business interactions. What he was missing, however, was the cultural wrapping.

That is precisely what Ms. Schwab so well represents in this very readable book. It's surely among the most useful, practical, and fun books on language acquisition any of us could read.

John K. Gillespie

President
Gillespie Global Group
New York, N.Y.
November 2019

はじめに

　言葉と文化が共有できたとき、人は海外でもコミュニケーション
ができます。このどちらが欠けても、相手に自分の意図を正確に伝
えることはできないのです。

　しゅわぶ美智子さんが触れられている、英語でのコミュニケー
ション術は、アメリカという日本とは異なったビジネス文化をもつ
環境で、いかに自分の意思を相手に伝えるかという意味において、極
めて有意義な示唆を与えてくれています。

　文化の違うさまざまな地域で相手との信頼関係を構築する究極の
方法は、まず失敗をおそれず、相手の文化に興味を持ち、その好奇
心を梃に積極性をもってその地域の人々と交流する姿勢をもつこと
です。そしてうまくいかなかった時は、どうしてなのか、相手のコ
ミュニケーションスタイルを熟知している人からのアドバイスに耳
を傾けることなのです。

　言語の達人ではなく、コミュニケーションの方法という一見目に
はみえないノウハウに視線を向けてみる姿勢が必要なのです。

　たとえば、日本人の「不可思議な笑み」という言葉があります。

　過去に、それは欧米の人々にとっては憧れの笑みであったことも
ありました。関東大震災でのことです。廃墟の中で食料の支援を待
つ人々が、笑みを浮かべながら列をつくってスープを待っている姿
に、西欧のメディアは好奇心を持ち、日本人の忍耐強く温かな表情
に憧れさえ抱いたのです。

　ところが、最近では、日本人が同じ笑みを浮かべるが故に、何を
考えているかわからないと批判されます。同じ意識と同じコミュニ
ケーションスタイルによって表れる笑みも、状況によって捉えられ
方が異なるのです。ステレオタイプへの警鐘はここにあります。

日本人は、英語を話すとき、自信がないことを笑みでごまかします。そして、ついつい視線も弱くなります。この「照れ笑い」が海外の人の多くからビジネスの現場での「不可解」な表情だと敬遠されます。しかし、廃墟の中で列をつくり、相手を気遣いながらついつい遠慮して浮かべる笑みは美しかったのです。ですから、決して自分の文化に対して卑屈になることはないのです。ただ、文化の異なる相手と接するときに、相手の文化背景に従ったコミュニケーションスタイルに合わせるスキルを作ることが大切なのです。その上で、自らの文化をいかに相手に知ってもらい、そこからお互いの文化の強さを合わせ、より強い知恵の交換ができるようにしてゆくことができるかが、グローバルな時代といわれる現在に求められているのです。

　しゅわぶ美智子さんが書かれた貴重なノウハウを活かしながら、お互いの文化の強みを合わせ、多様性を受け入れることで、さらに交流を深化させる知恵へとアップグレードしてゆくことが大切です。失敗を恐れず、失敗から偏見へと傾斜せず、お互いの異なる文化という2点を直線で結び、そこから正三角形のピラミッドを作ってゆければと思っているのです。

　異文化ビジネスコミュニケーションという言葉が語られてすでに長い年月が経過しています。しかし、私たちは今なお言葉さえ通じれば大丈夫だと思いがちです。そこに大きな落とし穴があり、ビジネスでの信頼関係に罅がはいることもままあります。相手がどうしてこのような反応をするのかなと思った瞬間に、まず彼らの長い歴史の中で、そして経験の中で培われてきた私たちとは異なる意思を伝達するノウハウがあることを察知しましょう。それが、ここで触れた正三角形のピラミッドを作ってゆく第一歩となるのです。

異文化ビジネスコンサルタント　山久瀬洋二

Table of Contents

目次

Author's Note

I wrote this book in English first and then translated it into Japanese. This is mainly because I found it difficult to write in Japanese while I was reflecting on various situations where the communication took place in English. Also, I knew from previous experience that I would have a more difficult time translating my Japanese into English than the other way around.

I have tried to match my Japanese translation to my English to the best of my abilities; however, please note that it is not a word-for-word translation. I wanted to convey the same meaning in both languages. Still, I know my efforts have fallen short in some places, and I am the one responsible for those shortcomings.

翻訳について

　私はこの本を、最初に英語で書き、その後日本語に翻訳しました。主な理由は、英語でコミュニケートした状況に思いを巡らしながら、日本語で書くことが難しかったからです。また、以前の経験から、日本語を英語に翻訳するのが、その逆に比べて大変だということを知っていました。

　日本語を原文の英語の意味にできる限り近づける努力をしましたが、逐訳ではないことをご了承願います。同じ意味を両方の言語でお伝えしたかったのですが、努力が実らなかったところもあります。至らない点は、すべて私の責任です。

For Walter

Thank you for reading my first draft and
giving me positive feedback.
Without your everlasting patience,
this book wouldn't have come into existence.

ウォルターへ

　最初の原稿のよい点を指摘してくれて、ありがとう。
アイデアを本にできたのは、あなたの忍耐強さのおかげです。

Dear Readers,

My field of work is called intercultural communication or cross-cultural communication. I help improve communication between Japanese and non-Japanese mostly in business at Japanese and non-Japanese companies, including American companies.

Intercultural communication is usually translated in Japanese as *i-bunka* (different culture) communication. Several of my Japanese clients said "I didn't want to come see you as '*i-bunka* training' sounded scary." This is probably because the Chinese character "*i* (異)" means "being different or strange," and doesn't sound friendly or approachable.

However, intercultural communication means communicating across cultures. In other words, it is crossing over the bridge to the other culture(s) or communicating between/among cultures. It is based on multiculturalism, which values each and every culture. This intercultural communication field is where trainers and coaches help people/companies improve and enhance their communication skills so that they can cultivate relationships with people from other cultures and reach their business goals, while respecting cultural differences.

When I started working as an intercultural trainer/coach more than twenty years ago, I thought my work would eventually disappear. Japanese would be exposed to and be connected with

読者の皆さまへ

　私の専門分野は、インターカルチュラル・コミュニケーション、またはクロスカルチュラル・コミュニケーションと呼ばれます。日本人と海外の人たちとのコミュニケーションを改善するサポートを、日本企業と海外の企業——アメリカ企業を含む——で行っています。

　インターカルチュラル・コミュニケーションは、日本語では「異文化コミュニケーション」と訳されます。以前、私のクライアントの中に「異文化トレーニング」はなんとなく怖くて、受講したくないという方が何人かいました。「異」という漢字に「違う、変わっている」という意味があることから、とっつきにくいと思われたのかもしれません。

　けれども「異文化コミュニケーション」とは、文化を超えてコミュニケーションすることなのです。「他の文化に通じる橋を渡る」、または「多文化間でコミュニケーションすること」と言い換えてもいいでしょう。異文化でのコミュニケーションは、それぞれの文化を尊重する「多文化主義」に基づいています。ですから、異文化トレーナーやコーチの役割は、文化の違いを認め合いながら、他文化の人と人間関係を築き、ビジネスで成果をあげられるようになるためのコミュニケーション・スキルの改善や向上を手助けすることなのです。

　二十年以上前に、異文化トレーナー、コーチとして働き始めたとき、この仕事はいずれなくなるだろうと思っていました。時がたてば、日本人はもっと世界に出ていき、海外とのネットワーク

the world and would become a more integrated part of the world. Based on my observations over the past twenty years, however, I have to admit that I was wrong about this.

This is probably because English education in Japan hasn't evolved much over the years. This doesn't help create opportunities to cultivate and deepen friendship/relationships with non-Japanese, and therefore it still limits the opportunity to share goals, working experiences and achievements with fellow non-Japanese.

One of the reasons I believe this is that I've heard the same comments on a regular basis for more than twenty years.

"I'm okay, because my colleagues know that Japanese don't speak English well."

"I can't speak English!"

"Native speakers of English should be able to guess what I mean."

"I have good intuition. I don't need to ask questions in English to learn what kind of people they are."

If you're a Japanese, you may agree or sympathize with these comments, and you may not worry too much about them. I'm afraid these comments have become ingrained in Japanese common sense. They seem innocent and benign. But they can be expressions of our subconscious thoughts about ourselves that limit us to our current status: spectators in the global arena.

を築き、より重要な世界の構成員になるだろうと思っていたからです。しかし残念ながら、私の予想は間違っていたと、今、認めざるをえません。

　海外の人と日本人のコミュニケーションが今でもうまくいかない理由。それは、日本の英語教育がこの間にあまり進化しなかったことが原因だと言えます。従来の日本の英語教育では、大人になってから、海外の人と友情や人間関係を築いたり深めたりする機会をつくるのは難しく、そのせいで、目標や共に働く経験、成果などを他文化の仲間と共有する機会も持ちにくいのです。

　私がこう考える理由の一つは、この二十年の間に以下のようなコメントを日本人から聞き続けてきたからです。

　「私は大丈夫、だって（アメリカ人の）同僚は日本人が英語を話せないのを知っているから」

　「英語が話せません！」

　「私が言いたいことを、ネイティブスピーカーはわかるはず」

　「私は勘がいいんです。彼ら（海外の人）がどんな人かを知るために、英語で質問する必要はありません」

　日本人なら、こういったコメントに同意したり共感したりするかもしれません。そして、たいして気にもとめないのでしょう。残念ながら、このようなコメントは、日本人の常識になってしまったようです。無邪気で無害な発言のように思えます。しかしこれらは、私たち日本人を現状——つまりグローバルフィールドの観客席——にとどめている、無意識の思いを表現したものに思えます。

My idea for this book started to take shape when I began to think about what could help us walk onto the global playing field and get involved in whatever game we want to play.

You may be thinking "What's the big deal about these comments?" So, let's examine them and see how they can be fraught with risks of misunderstanding.

■ Common Japanese Comments [1]

I'm okay, because my colleagues know that Japanese don't speak English well.

Let's imagine that you said the same thing about your Japanese language ability: "I'm okay, because my Japanese colleagues know that I don't speak Japanese well." Now, you're excluding yourself from the conversation, and possibly isolating yourself from the group that you are or need to be a part of. This situation is no different when the language is English. Besides, it's hard to earn respect from people when you ask for special treatment.

If a young student says, "I'm okay, because my teachers know that I don't do well in school." What would you say to him or her? "Please don't give up on yourself."

Also, this comment makes it sound as if all Japanese have the same issue, encouraging others to stereotype Japanese. That is not very helpful or fair to those Japanese who are trying hard!

どうすれば日本人が観客席からグローバルフィールドに降り
ていき、自分のゲームをプレイするようになれるのだろうかと考
え始めたとき、この本の輪郭が見えてきました。

　もしかすると、「このコメントの何が問題なんだ？」と思われる
かもしれません。ですので、一つひとつを検証して、これらのコ
メントに潜む誤解の危険性を見てみましょう。

■ よくある日本人のコメント[1]

私は大丈夫、だって同僚は日本人が英語をうまく話せないのを知ってますから

　同じことを、あなたの日本語能力について言ったとしましょ
う。「私は大丈夫、だって日本人の同僚は私が日本語をうまく話
せないのを知ってますから」　この場合、あなたは自分を対話か
ら除外していることになり、あなたが属するまたは属する必要の
あるグループから自分を孤立させることになりかねません。この
状況は、言語が英語でも同じです。また、特別扱いを頼んでおき
ながら、その人にあなたを尊重してもらうのは難しいです。

　もし年少の生徒が、「大丈夫、だって私の先生は、私が勉強が
苦手なのを知っているから」と言ったら、あなたはその子に何と
言いますか？「諦めないで」と言うのではないでしょうか。

　また、このコメントは、あたかも日本人全員が同じ問題を抱え
ているかのように聞こえるので、海外の人に日本人に関する間
違った固定観念を植えつけてしまうかもしれません。それでは、
一生懸命頑張っている日本人の助けになりませんし、彼らの評判
を不当に下げかねません。

I can't speak English!

Many non-Japanese are bewildered by this comment. "But didn't you learn English in school?" many of them ask. "Don't you want to improve your English?" many of them wonder. Many non-Japanese may be lenient for a while about your lack of conversational English skills. But not for long. If you keep saying this, you may appear as if justifying your lack of effort or even bragging about it, and they may conclude that you're refusing to talk with non-Japanese. As you can imagine, it'll become very difficult to cultivate trusting relationships.

Native speakers of English should be able to guess what I mean.

As a nation, we're a people who don't want to cause others trouble as the result of what we do. But somehow, some of us don't mind asking non-Japanese to "guess what I mean by listening to my imperfect English." This puts a lot of burden on non-Japanese. They don't want to have to make wild guesses about what you may be saying, and some of them may start avoiding you.

英語が話せません！

　海外の人の多くは、このコメントに困惑します。「でも、学校で英語を習いませんでした？」と聞いてきます。「英語を上達したいと思わないの？」といぶかります。海外の人たちは最初のうちは私たちの会話スキルの低さに寛容です。しかし、長くは続きません。もし「英語が話せません」を言い続けると、自分の努力不足を正当化したり、それを自慢しているかのようにさえ聞こえてきます。あなたが海外の人と話すのを拒否していると判断されてしまうかもしれません。想像できると思いますが、こうなるとお互いに信用できる人間関係を築くのは難しくなってしまいます。

私が言いたいことを、ネイティブ・スピーカーはわかるはず

　日本は、他人に迷惑をかけたくないと思っている人が多い国です。ところが、「私の不十分な英語を聞いて、私の言いたいことを推測してください」と頼むことにためらいを感じない日本人もいます。これは相手にとっては重荷です。あなたの言っていることを当てずっぽうに推測したくないので、あなたを避け始める人もでてきます。

I have good intuition. I don't need to ask questions in English to learn what kind of people they are.

Human communication is full of nuances. Therefore, there are always misunderstandings, even among native speakers of any language. So, while you may find your hunch very helpful to you, it comes with risks that could also harm your communication and reputation.

Please know that I'm not criticizing individuals who have made these comments. They didn't make these statements with any bad intentions; they were merely sharing their honest feelings. But I find these statements very alarming, because most Japanese have no idea about the implications of these comments (i.e., why such comments are not accepted anywhere else in the world). So, how can we express the same sentiments in a way non-Japanese find acceptable?

◆ Path to Mastery 1

"Please bear with me, I'll try my best to explain myself," instead of "I'm okay, because my colleagues know that Japanese don't speak English well."

"I'll improve my English!" instead of "I can't speak English!"

"How can I say this in a way that others can understand

私は勘がいいんです。彼ら（海外の人）がどんな人かを知るために、英語で質問する必要はありません

　人のコミュニケーションにはニュアンスがたくさん含まれているので、同じ言語を母国語とする人たちの中でさえ、誤解が絶えません。ですから、今まで勘に助けられたことが何度もあったとしても、勘だけに頼っていると、あなたのコミュニケーションと評判を損なうリスクが生じます。

　このようなコメントをした人たちには悪意はなく、正直な思いを伝えてくれただけだということはわかっていますし、私は、彼らを非難しているわけではありません。けれども、このようなコメントが海外ではどのように解釈されるか（つまり、どうしてこのようなコメントが海外では受け入れられないか）をほとんどの日本人が気づいていない点が、非常に気がかりなのです。では、同じ思いを海外の人に抵抗なく受け入れてもらえるようにするには、どうすればよいのでしょうか？

⟡ コミュニケーションの極意 1

　　私は大丈夫、だって同僚は日本人が英語をうまく話せないのを知っているから

　　　　⇒我慢して聞いてください。ベストを尽くして説明しますから

　　英語が話せません！

　　　　⇒英語が上達するよう頑張ります

me?" instead of "Native speakers of English should be able to guess what I mean."

"I won't pretend that I understand others until I listen to and understand what they're actually saying," instead of "I have good intuitions. I don't need to ask questions in English to learn what kind people they are."

In other words, we have to change the conversation about English that we've been having with ourselves.

I agree that learning a foreign language is a big challenge. But please remember, speaking English isn't a game where you show off your intelligence. It's a tool to expand your understanding of others, as well as the world, to expand your horizons and enrich your life. Therefore, your will to speak up is more important than your desire to speak it perfectly. We learned English for at least six years as part of our mandatory education. We have a good foundation for further learning. So, how can we leverage that education?

This book is my response to that question. I sincerely hope that the following pages will inspire and encourage you to get on the field and participate in the English-speaking world.

Michiko Schwab

私が言いたいことを、ネイティブ・スピーカーはわかるはず
　　➡これをどう言えば、人にわかってもらえるのでしょう？

私は勘がいいんです。彼ら（海外の人）がどんな人かを知るために、英語で質問する必要はありません
　　➡相手の話をしっかり聞いて内容を理解するまで、人のことをわかったフリをしません

　言い換えると、英語について私たちが心の中でしてきた会話を変える必要があるのです。
　外国語を学ぶのは、大きなチャレンジです。けれども、英語を話すのは、あなたの知性をひけらかすためのゲームではありません。英会話は、世界や海外の人への理解を広げるとともに深め、あなたの見識を広げ、人生を豊かにするためのツールです。ですから、完璧な英語を話したいという願いよりも、話す意欲の方がずっと大切です。私たちは義務教育の一環として、少なくとも六年間、英語を習いました。私たちにはより高い英語力を目指すための、十分な基礎力があります。では、この教育をうまく生かすには、どうすればいいのでしょう？
　本書は、この質問に対する私の返答です。この本が、あなたに気づきと勇気を与え、英語を話す世界へと飛び出し、がっぷり四つに組む助けとなることを心より願います。

　　　　　　　　　　　　　　　　　しゅわぶ美智子

Chapter I

Why Is Speaking English So Challenging for Japanese?

Listening culture vs. speaking culture

When I relocated from Tokyo, Japan, to a small, U.S. town near Phoenix, Arizona, and started learning English with fellow non-native speakers of English at a nearby community college, I was surprised that everyone else was able to speak English, even if it was only broken English. The teacher liked me because I tried to speak with the correct grammar, but I envied other students.

Clearly, their problem (grammar) and my problem (not being able to use what I knew) were different. But every human being is equipped with language ability, and my classmates seemed able to apply their skills of speaking their native language to speaking English. Then, why couldn't I do

第1章

日本人が英語で話すのは、
どうして難しいの？

聞く文化と話す文化

　東京からアメリカのアリゾナ州フェニックス市の近くにある小さな町に引っ越した私は、近くのコミュニティ・カレッジで他の外国人と一緒に英語を学び始めました。そのときびっくりしたのは、私以外の人はみな、曲がりなりにも英語を話せたことでした。文法を気にして話したので、先生には気に入られましたが、私は他の人がうらやましくてしかたありませんでした。

　明らかに、他の生徒さんたちの問題（文法）と私の問題（知っている英語の知識を生かせない）は違いました。けれども、人間はだれでも言語を学ぶ能力を持っています。他の生徒は、母国語を話すときに使っているスキルを、英語を話すときに生かしているようでした。どうして私には、できなかったのでしょうか？ 日本

the same thing? Why is speaking English so challenging for Japanese, when we have a strong foundation of grammar and vocabulary?

Most Japanese I have met in the US, both in business and outside of work, share the same observation. So, I've reached the conclusion that something beyond the innate language ability that we all possess, namely Japanese culture, is somehow holding us back. One big factor is our focus on listening. Japanese society encourages us to become adept listeners but not necessarily excellent speakers. Japanese listening culture is well expressed in the proverb "Listen to one and understand ten."

"The duck that quacks gets shot" means that you don't want to cause trouble for yourself by saying unnecessary things.

However, in my English class in Arizona, students from Mexico, Latin America, and other Asian countries spoke without hesitation and with ease. They seemed to be relaxed about speaking English. When I wanted to speak, however, I needed to summon all of my courage and jump into the conversation, as if I were plunging off a cliff into water far below. I wanted to acquire the same relaxed attitude toward speaking English, but of course, the more I tried to relax, the more tense I became. So, I assumed that my classmates' attitude toward English was based on their attitude toward their native language, and it was natural for them to speak up whenever they wanted to do so.

人には英語の文法と語彙のしっかりした基礎がありながら、どうして英語を話すのが難しいのでしょう？

　アメリカで仕事や他の機会を通じて出会った日本人の多くは、私と同じように感じています。そのことから私は、生まれながらの言語能力を超えた何か、つまり「日本の文化」が私たちの英会話能力の開発を妨げているという結論に達しました。大きな要因の一つは、私たちが「聞く」ことを大切にすることです。日本の社会はよい聞き手になることを勧めますが、素晴らしい話し手になることを必ずしも求めません。日本の聞く文化は、「一を聞いて十を知る」のことわざによく表れています。

　また、「雉も鳴かずば撃たれまい」は、余計なことを言って災いを招かないほうがよいという意味のことわざです。
　しかし私が受けた英語の授業では、メキシコ、ラテン・アメリカ諸国、他のアジア諸国から来た生徒が、何のためらいもなく気軽に話していました。彼らは英語を話すことを気楽に考えているようでした。でも、私が話そうと思うと、清水の舞台から飛び降りるかのように、勇気を振り絞って会話に飛び込まなければなりませんでした。彼らと同じような、くつろいだ姿勢を身につけたかったのですが、力を抜こうとすればするほど緊張してしまうのです。見たところ、彼らの英語に対する姿勢は、彼らの母国語に対する姿勢からくるもので、話したいときに話すのが当たり前と考えているようでした。

Later I also learned that in most Western cultures, especially immigrant nations like the U.S., Canada, England, and Australia, speaking is actually considered a great skill and a sign of intelligence. These countries are also the Western countries whose basic philosophy is based on Socrates, a Greek philosopher from the 5th century BC who used a wide range of discussions to seek the true nature of things. Besides, in these countries, which are more open to accepting immigrants than Japan, people with different cultural backgrounds, education, belief systems, ideas, and ways of thinking live and work together. Therefore, the ability to speak and discuss ideas and opinions with others is of paramount importance. This is a huge difference from the more homogenous Japanese culture where being attentive and anticipating others' wishes without asking questions is a virtue, and speaking skills are of less importance.

Group-oriented culture and individualistic culture

The next difference that I noticed was that Americans knew themselves much better than I knew myself. If you live in an individualistic society like the U.S., you have been asked two kinds of questions since you were very little—say, four years old. These questions are:

その後、西欧諸国の多く、特に移民が多いアメリカとカナダ、イギリス、オーストラリアでは、話すのは重要なスキルであり、知性の表れとも考えられていることを知りました。これらの国は、広範囲の討論を通じて物事の本質を追求した、紀元前5世紀のギリシャの哲学者、ソクラテスの哲学を踏襲している西側諸国です。また、これらの国々では、日本に比べ移民の受け入れ態勢が整っていて、その結果、さまざまな文化的な生い立ちや教育、宗教、アイデア、考え方の人たちがともに暮らし、働いています。ですから、アイデアや意見について話したり議論したりする能力は、何にもまして重要です。これは、より同質的な文化の中で、質問をせずに相手を思いやり、相手の心を察するのが美徳であり、また話すスキルがそれほど重要視されない日本とは非常に大きな違いです。

グループを大切にする文化と個人を大切にする文化

　次に私が気づいた違いは、彼らは自分のことを非常によく知っているということでした。アメリカのような個人を大切にする文化の中で暮らすと、まだ幼い4歳ぐらいのころから次の二つの質問を聞きながら育ちます。

"What do you think?"

"Why do you think so?"

Of course, when you were four years old, the questions you were asked are something like, "What do you like to drink?" and "What do you want to play with?" But little children start learning to decide based on their feelings and opinions. Children in the Western world are on their journey of self-discovery from the get-go. This creates a big difference over time. Grown-ups in the Western world may not know what others are thinking; however, they know a great deal about themselves. Their preferred logic, what they like and dislike, their goals, and their dreams. Knowing who you are as an individual gives you a certain confidence. I think this is one of the reasons why Westerners can express their ideas and opinions with great confidence.

In Japan, however, these two questions have less importance. We are much more interested in the "how" than what and why. Typically, at home and in school, parents and teachers don't ask children "What do you think?" and "Why do you think so?" When adult Japanese tell children to do something, the children assume that it is something necessary to get done (what) and don't ask the adults for reasons (why). Or the answers to these questions are readily provided by parents and teachers in the instructions, so that the children can focus on the "how." If a Japanese child asks for reasons for a task, he or

「あなたはどう思う？」

　「どうして、そう思うの？」

　もちろん、４歳のときに聞かれる質問は、「何飲みたい？」「何して遊びたい？」といったものです。しかし小さいころから、子どもたちは自分の気持ちや考えに基づいて物事を決めることを学びます。欧米諸国の子どもたちは、自己発見の道を歩み始めるのです。時間がたつにつれ、これは大きな違いを生みます。欧米の大人は、他人が何を考えているかは知らないかもしれません。しかし、自分自身のことは非常によく知っています。自分の好きな論理、好きなもの嫌いなもの、自分の目標と夢。自分がどんな人間かがわかっていると、ある種の自信が生まれます。これは、欧米人が自分のアイデアと意見を、自信たっぷりに表現できる理由の一つだと思います。

　一方日本では、この二つの質問はあまり大切ではありません。私たちは「何」と「なぜ」より、「やり方」のほうに興味があります。家庭でも学校でも、親も先生も「どう思う？」と「どうしてそう思うの？」という質問を投げかけません。大人が子どもに指示をすると、子どもたちはそれをしあげなければならないものだ（何）とみなし、それが必要な理由（なぜ）を尋ねません。もしくは、それらの質問に対する答えが、親や先生からの指示のなかに含まれていて、子どもたちは「やり方」に集中できるようになっているのです。日本では、子どもが作業をする理由を尋ねると、「難しい子」というレッテルを貼られてしまいます。

she will be labeled as "a difficult child."

Once I had brunch with several American friends, and each of them said, "I'll order this salad, because I like asparagus." "I'll have poached eggs, because I like eggs." "Oh, I'll have the carbonara because I like pasta." American schools and society really trained them well on the "what and why" way of thinking. I found it amusing because Japanese usually keep these comments to themselves, as we don't think others are interested in each person's reasoning.

In general, Japanese and other Asians are more outward-focused than people in the Western world. We want to take care of others and we pay more attention to how others may be feeling. We also tend to be more attuned to others' feelings. Ironically, we can sometimes talk about others' feelings based on our observations and experiences with them, but we don't know what we are feeling ourselves or can't articulate those feelings with words.

Also, Japanese are risk averse. We're afraid that our mistakes may have an impact on the group in which we belong. So, we tend to wait until we're really sure. As a result, we often miss the timing to join a conversation or delay our response to a question that was asked. We need to become less risk-averse and to share our thoughts before we are 100 percent sure.

あるとき、アメリカ人の友だちとブランチをともにしました。皆、「私、このサラダを注文するわ。アスパラが好きだから」「私はポーチドエッグ、卵好きだから」「私はパスタが好きだから、カルボナーラ」と言いました。アメリカの社会と学校で「何」と「なぜ」を中心とした考え方を叩きこまれているからです。私はこの違いを面白く感じました。日本人は、人が自分の理由に興味があるとは思わないので、通常、このようなコメントは控えます。

　一般に、日本人を含むアジア人は、欧米人に比べると他人を中心とした考え方をします。周りの人の面倒を見たいですし、人が何を感じているかを気にかけます。また、人の気持ちを感じとるのにも長けています。ですが皮肉なことに、自分の見立てと相手との経験に基づいて、人の気持ちを話すことはできるのに、自分自身の気持ちがよくわからなかったり、言葉ではっきりと表現できなかったりします。

　また、日本人はリスクを回避したがります。自分の間違いがグループに与える影響を心配します。それで、本当に確実になるまで、待ってしまいがちです。その結果、対話に参加する機会を逃してしまったり、質問に対する返事を遅らせてしまいがちです。私たちはもっとリスク回避を減らし、100パーセント確実になるのを待たずに、自分の考えを伝える必要があります。

Analogue and digital modes of communication

I learned about the concept of analogue vs. digital modes from Professor Kichiro Hayashi in graduate school at Aoyama Gakuin, Tokyo, Japan. He explains that a digital clock can clearly show when it becomes one o'clock. In comparison, the second hand of an analogue clock moves continuously and can't really show the exact moment, say, when it becomes one o'clock.

For me, analogue is like the edge of the fog. You can tell the difference between when you're surrounded by fog and when there is no fog. But can you say exactly where the fog ends? Can you draw a clear line between the foggy area and the non-foggy area? It's not that easy because fog seems to come and go. Japanese can live with this kind of gray area. We actually use this kind of analogue perception, which allows us to have undefined or expanded time and space, to maintain harmony among ourselves. However, this can be very challenging to deal with for Westerners, and it can even annoy them.

Let me explain how the analogue mode works. In the spring we admire cherry blossoms by saying, "Oh, they're beautiful," and we assume that we're all feeling pretty much the same thing. If we start examining each other's thoughts and ask, "What are you thinking?" those answers may separate us. Someone may be thinking about why the beauty of cherry

アナログ・モードとデジタル・モードのコミュニケーション

　青山学院大学の大学院で、林吉郎教授からアナログ・モードとデジタル・モードのコンセプトを学びました。デジタル時計は、たとえば1時になる瞬間をはっきりと示します。一方、アナログ時計の秒針の動きには連続性があり、1時になる瞬間を正確には示さないというのです。

　私にとって、アナログは霧の境界線のようなものです。霧に囲まれているときと、霧のない状態との違いはわかります。でも、霧がどこで終わるか正確に示せますか？　霧に囲まれている領域とそうでない領域との間に明確な線を引けますか？　霧はどこからともなく来て消えるので、簡単に線を引けません。日本人は、これに似たあいまいさの中でも生活できます。また、時空をきっちり定義しない、または時空の柔軟な伸び縮みを可能にするアナログ認識を使って、調和を保ちます。しかし欧米人は、このあいまいさを含むコミュニケーションが苦手で、イライラしてしまうのです。

　アナログ・モードがどのように働くのか、説明しましょう。春になると、日本人は桜を見て「あぁ、きれいだねぇ」と言い、みながだいたい同じように感じていると思い込みます。それぞれの人の考えを見極めようと、「何を考えてるの？」と聞き始めると、ばらばらな返答のせいで、お互いの距離感を感じてしまうかもしれません。中には、「どうして桜の花の美しさにそれほど強く惹か

blossoms captures her or his heart so strongly. Another person may be thinking, "Will the cherry blossoms still be beautiful over the weekend when I play golf?" Or "I want to have a party with my friends under the cherry trees at the nearby park." But we don't express those thoughts right there and then, because we prefer to enjoy the shared feelings rather than show the differences of our thoughts.

On the other hand, the digital mode of communication is very clear, and you're often asked to choose between two options, like the following:

Yes or no
Agree or disagree
Pass or fail
For here or to go
 (eating a meal at the store, or taking it somewhere else to eat)

Sparkling water or regular water
Salad or soup
Like or dislike (not like)
Guilty or not guilty

Sometimes it is hard to pick one over the other, as we use a lot of gray area in Japanese communication. We might say, "I'm not sure," or, "Well, it depends" or, "I'll think about it." It's not that you always have to decide right away. But if you say "I'm not sure" too many times, people with the digital

れるのだろう」と考えている人もいるでしょう。「今週末にゴルフ
をするときまで、桜の花が咲いているだろうか」、もしくは、「近
くの公園の桜の木の下で友だちとお花見をしたいなぁ」と思って
いるかもしれません。けれども日本人はそういった考えをその場
ではっきりと口にしません。それは私たちが考えの違いを明らか
にするよりも、共感することを好むからです。

　一方、デジタル・モードのコミュニケーションの特徴は明確さ
で、以下にあげるような二つの選択肢のどちらかを選ぶように求
められます。

　　イエスかノーか
　　同意か反対か
　　合格か落第(基準到達か失敗)か
　　店の中で食べるか、持ち帰るか

　　スパークリング・ウォーターか普通の水か
　　サラダかスープか
　　好きか嫌いか
　　有罪か無罪か

　日本人どうしのコミュニケーションでは、ぼかした表現を使う
ことが多いので、英語で聞かれた二者択一の質問に答えるのが難
しいときもあります。そんなとき、「ちょっとわからないです」と
か、「場合によります」とか、「考えてみます」と答えがちです。け
れども「ちょっとわかりません」をくり返しすぎると、デジタル・

mode may get frustrated and assume that you can't think or you're not willing to share what you're actually thinking. They may even come away with the impression that you're indecisive, dishonest, or sneaky. So, it may be a good idea to choose one quickly if the question is not about something critical, and is simply something you can live with either way, like, "Coffee or tea?" or "Red or white wine?"

Languages are like music

I like music—almost all types, but I can't find a way to enjoy rap music. To me, the rhythm of rap music seems to be a bit behind the beat and that bothers me. Because I'm not comfortable with rap music's rhythm, I can't even focus on the message (melody). I think that music and language have a lot in common. Every human has a primary language, whether spoken or sign language. But speaking another language can be very different because some of the elements are not the same as our native language. This is exactly why even if you can "read" music, it may not translate directly into the ability to perform the music. So even if I could read rap music on paper, if I were to play it in my natural way, nobody would recognize it as rap music. However, over time I could learn how to make it sound more like rap music. And this has already happened to the English language, and there are many versions of English in the world. What we need to do isn't necessarily to become a

モードの人は不満を募らせ、あなたのことを考える能力がない
か、もしくは自分の本当の考えを人に教えたくないのだと、決め
てかかるかもしれません。ですから、質問の内容が重要なもので
はなく、「コーヒーか紅茶？」「赤ワインか白ワイン？」のような、
どちらでもいいと思えるものの場合、どちらかをさっさと選ぶの
が得策です。

言語は音楽に似ている

　私はほとんどすべてのジャンルの音楽が好きですが、ラップ・
ミュージックにはどうしても馴染めません。ラップ・ミュージッ
クのリズムはビートに乗り遅れているように聞こえて、すっきり
しないのです。ラップ・ミュージックのリズムが居心地が悪いの
で、メッセージ（メロディ）から気がそれてしまいます。音楽と
言語には共通点がたくさんあります。音を使うのであれ手話であ
れ、どの人にも第一言語があります。しかし、第一言語と各要素
の内容が違う別の言語を話すのは、また違った経験です。楽譜を
「読む」ことができても、その音楽を演奏できるとは限りません。
ラップ・ミュージックの楽譜を読めたとしても、私が自分なりの
やり方で歌ったら、それがラップ・ミュージックとは誰も思わな
いでしょう。けれど、時間をかけて習えば、ラップ・ミュージッ
クらしく歌えるようになるでしょう。これは、英語の世界で実際
に起きていることです。世界にはいろんなバージョンの英語があ
ります。私たちに必要なのは、ネイティブ・スピーカーになるこ
とではなく、世界の人たちにわかってもらえるバージョンの英語

native speaker, but to develop our version of English that other English speakers in the world can understand.

I think language is like music, and that the difficulty we have in speaking English has less to do with words and grammar, but more to do with how to coordinate the many different elements and orchestrate them to speak. According to Melissa Runhart, there are seven elements in music:

7 Elements of Music		7 Elements of Spoken English
1	Rhythm	When to speak, when to listen
2	Melody	Message
3	Harmony	The degree of tolerance towards difference and disagreement
4	Timbre (Tone color)	Attitude
5	Form	Grammar
6	Texture	Relationships
7	Dynamics	Speaking slow or fast, volume, and pitch

■ 7 Elements [1]

When to speak, when to listen (Rhythm)

Japanese language has its own rhythm, which allows for moments of silence and pauses. We don't have to be constantly talking. Silence or a pause can be a sign of respect, consideration, disagreement, or simply being polite. The Japanese sense of hierarchy also plays a role here. When you're speaking with someone who is above you, you're

を身につけることです。

　言語は音楽と似ています。私たちが英語を話すときに感じる難しさは単語や文法よりも、多くの違った要素を組み合わせて、話すという動作にまとめあげることにあります。メリッサ・ランハート*によると、音楽には7つの要素があります。

	音楽の7要素	英語で話す
1	リズム	いつ話し、いつ聞くか
2	メロディ／旋律	メッセージ
3	調和	違いや意見の対立への寛容さ
4	音色	態度
5	形式	文法
6	質感(旋律と和音による構成)	関係
7	ダイナミックス(強弱法)	話す速さ、音量と音の高低

■ 7つの要素 [1]

いつ話し、いつ聞くか──リズム

　日本語の会話には、短い沈黙の後や一息ついてから話し始める独特のリズムがあります。日本語の会話では、話が多少途切れてもかまいません。沈黙や相手が話したあとの一息の間は、相手に対する尊重や思いやり、意見の違い、または丁寧さの表れです。

＊メリッサ・ランハート：Melissa Runhart

expected to demonstrate silence (pause) as a way of showing your effort to understand and reflect on what you've just heard from your higher-ranking counterpart. The following shows a typical rhythm in a conversation between two Japanese of different hierarchal levels. "····" indicates the duration that a person speaks, and the spaces identify when there is silence. In the conversation below, person A is above person B in the hierarchy. Even when several people are involved in a conversation, the same kind of rhythm is maintained.

However, English has a different rhythm that encourages an immediate response, and it's not uncommon that you will hear multiple responses from several people at the same time. This is partly because the main point can be made in the first few words of the sentence. As soon as you hear someone talk in English, you'll immediately understand his or her position; agree, disagree, needs more data, expects an improvement, and so on.

In that rhythm, if you don't share your thoughts immediately, they may see you as a person who is not very honest, not trusting of others, or is hiding something. So, keeping your opinions to yourself for too long is not a good idea. You need to respond immediately, and show your willingness to participate in the conversation. The following shows a typical American rhythm in a conversation where several people are involved. Although hierarchy exists in the Western world too, they don't

日本人の上下関係に対する感覚も関係してきます。自分よりも上の役職の人と話すときは、相手から聞いた内容を理解し、そのことについて熟考しようとしているのを表現するのに、沈黙（間）が使われます。下の図は、上下関係に差のある日本人二人が話しているときの、典型的なリズムを表しています。「‥‥」は人が話していることを、空白は沈黙を表します。この会話では、AさんがBさんより上の立場です。数人で話しているときも、同じようなリズムが守られます。

A
（日本人）　　‥‥‥‥‥　　　‥‥‥‥‥‥‥　　　　‥‥‥‥‥‥‥‥　　　‥‥‥‥‥

B
（日本人）　　　　　‥‥‥‥　　　　　‥‥‥‥‥‥‥　　　　　‥‥‥‥

　しかし、英語では即座の返答を求められるので、リズムが違ってきます。数人から同時に返答がくることも珍しくありません。これは、英語では文の最初の数単語で言いたいポイントを表現できることと関係しています。誰かが英語で話し始めると、賛成、反対、もっとデータが必要、改善を期待するなど、その人の見解がすぐに理解できます。
　英語のリズムでは、自分の考えをすぐに表明しないと、あなたがあまり正直でないとか、人を信用しないとか、何かを隠しているなどと思われかねません。ですから、自分の考えを長い間話さずにいるのはよくありません。すぐに相手に返答し、対話に参加する意欲を見せるようにしましょう。次頁の図は、数人のアメリカ人が話すときの典型的なリズムを表しています。欧米でも上下関係は存在しますが、あまりこだわりません。誰かが話し終わらないうちに他の人が話し始めても、また、同じグループの中で一

usually pay much attention to it. It is okay to talk over each other, and to have a separate conversation within a group. In the following diagram, five people are in a discussion. Person A raised the subject, and then person C led it for a while. Person B only spoke a little, and Persons D and E had a side conversation. At the end, person D spoke to the entire group and the others listened.

■ 7 Elements [2]
Message (Melody)

Japanese often fail to deliver the message in English. It is partly because of the different rhythm that I mentioned above. A more important factor, though, is how you deliver the message, or the sequence.

Japanese culture is based more on similarity. Basically, we have one educational system, share the same time zone, and speak one language. This creates an environment where we don't have to say things clearly each time in order for us to

部の人が別の話をしてもかまいません。

　左の図では、五人が討議を行っています。Ａさんが話題を出し、Ｃさんがしばらく話をリードします。Ｂさんが少しだけ話すと、ＤさんとＥさんが二人だけで個別の話をします。終わりには、Ｄさんが全員に向かって話し、他の人たちは聞き手に回ります。

メッセージ──メロディ

　日本人が英語で話すとき、往々にして、メッセージを伝えそびれてしまいます。その原因の一つは、上記のリズムの違いです。しかし、より重要な要因はメッセージの伝え方、つまり話の組み立て方です。

　日本の文化は似ている点に注目して話す文化です。基本的に日本の教育システムは一つですし、タイム・ゾーンも一つ、そして同じ言語を話します。日本は、言いたいことを毎回明確に伝えなくても、お互いを理解し合える環境なのです。

understand each other.

In conversation, too, similarities come before differences. For example, we tend to confirm things that we can agree on. Or, we talk about things in common between conversation partners, and then move onto the main subject or raise an issue for discussion. Westerners, however, are more interested in differences. They feel if there are differences in ideas and opinions, then it's worth talking about them. Otherwise, the conversation may be boring. Therefore, you need to skip the section on similarities and go right to the point in order to keep their attention.

When Japanese speak among ourselves, we talk less about the reasons why something is important enough to talk about. It is usually obvious to us, or we have learned about it through informal meetings or at least we've guessed it more or less through assessing the situations that have been developing around us. So, we tend to confirm the situation first and then skip "what" and "why" and jump to talking about the "how." On the other hand, Westerners are first and foremost interested in the reasons why a particular subject is worth their time. Even when people have the same point, each person's view and reason can differ. That makes the conversation interesting. Listening to each other's reasoning helps them understand each person's role, character, view point, preferred logic, and so on. This process also helps them strengthen their connection with their friends and colleagues.

日本人は対話でも、まず類似点について話し、それから相違点の話に移行します。たとえば、同意し合える点をまず確認します。または、相手との共通点について話してから、主要な案件に移ったり、討議事項を提案したりします。しかし欧米人は、違う点にこそ興味があります。彼らにとっては、アイデアや意見に違いがあればこそ、話し合う価値があるのです。そうでなければ、退屈な対話になってしまいます。ですから、欧米人の注意を引きつけるには、似ている点はあと回しにして、自分が一番伝えたい点をまず述べる必要があります。

　日本人どうしで話すとき、その話題や案件がどうして重要なのか、理由をあまり説明しません。たいていの場合、理由が明らかか、私的な情報交換を通じてすでに知っているか、少なくとも周りの状況の変化から判断しておおよその見当をつけています。ですから、状況をまず確認した後は「何」と「なぜ」を飛ばして、「解決方法」について話します。ところが欧米人にとって一番興味があるのは、なぜ特定の案件に時間を費やす価値があるのかです。結論が同じ人たちの間でも、それぞれの見方や理由が違うことがあります。それが、対話を面白くするのです。お互いの理由を聞く中で、各人の役割や性格、観点、好みの考え方などの理解が深まります。また、このプロセスを経る中で、友人や同僚との絆が強まるのです。

The main point → Reason

If you want to keep your non-Japanese audience engaged in a conversation, you need to present your point and then give reasons, all in a timely fashion. And then, you can share your experiences that support your reasons. Your examples can show who you are, and your conversation partners can get to know you more on a personal level.

The main point → Reason → Example

It's nearly impossible to get through this process in English in one fell swoop, because English rhythm allows your conversation partners to interrupt you and add their comments or ask questions. But you can also interrupt others and go back to what you want to say. This is fair game in the Western world. So, please don't get discouraged just because you couldn't finish your thoughts with your first try. Grab a chance to take the stage back to your topic, and continue where you left off.

Useful Expression

1. I know exactly what you're saying, that is why … (share your point and reasons)

2. I know how you feel. I had a similar experience, when … (share your examples)

3. I agree with you. Maybe we should talk about … (adding a comment on the point/conclusion)

ポイント → 理由

　海外の人を対話に引きつけておきたいなら、伝えたいポイントをまず伝えて、次にタイミングを逃さずに理由を述べます。それから、理由を納得してもらうために、あなたの経験（例）を伝えます。あなたの経験にはあなたらしさが表れ、対話の相手は、個人としてのあなたをもっと知ることができます。

ポイント → 理由 → 例

　この一連の流れを一気に完了するのはほぼ不可能です。なぜなら英語のリズムが、対話の相手があなたの話を遮り、自分の発言を加えたり質問をしたりしやすくするからです。けれども、あなたも相手の話を遮って、自分が話したい内容に相手を引き戻すことができます。これは欧米では、対話の公正なやり方と考えられています。ですから、一回で最後まで話し終えることができなくても、やる気をなくさないでください。あなたの話題にスポットライトを戻すチャンスをつかみ、前に話が途切れたところに戻って、話し続けましょう。

使える表現

1. あなたの言っていること、わかります。だから私も……（あなたのポイントと理由を話します）

2. お気持ちわかります。私も似たような経験があります。あれは……（あなたの例を話します）

3. 同感です。……について話しましょう……（相手のポイントや結論に追加のコメントをします）

The degree of tolerance towards difference and disagreement (Harmony)

In my view, Japanese have a unique definition of harmony that contradicts itself. In music, harmony implies that many tones are coming together as music. However, when a Japanese group is harmonious, it usually means that they agree on one thing and suppress other opinions. So, it appears to be harmonious, but in reality, it may be a forced monotone, and therefore is not true harmony. In general, Japanese don't have much tolerance towards different opinions, because maintaining the appearance of harmony is of paramount importance. So, in Japan, the land where "harmony is valued," people don't express different voices, as the Japanese definition of harmony is one voice or consensus created by controlling dissenting opinions. It's rather contradictory if you look at it from a non-Japanese point of view.

When I ask Westerners to define "harmony" they usually say something like "to have many voices in a group, playing/ working together towards a common goal." So, it implies inclusiveness that allows space for different opinions, although they have to deal with certain disagreements and uncomfortableness coming from those different opinions.

違いや意見の対立への寛容度──ハーモニー

　日本人のハーモニー（調和）の定義は、自己矛盾する独特なものだと、私は思っています。音楽では、複数の音が一緒になって音楽を作り出すとハーモニー（調和）が生まれます。しかし、日本人のグループが調和の状態にある場合、通常、皆が一つのことに同意し、他の意見が抑制されていることを意味します。ですから、見た目には和が保たれていますが、それは強制的な単音ですから、本当の調和とは言えません。表面的な和を維持することが非常に大切なので、一般に、違う意見に対する日本人の寛容度は高くありません。日本人の和の定義はハーモニーではなく単音、つまり反対意見を抑制して作られたコンセンサス（グループ内の合意）なのです。「和をもって尊しとす」の国、日本では、コンセンサスに合わない意見を表立って述べません。海外の人の目で見ると、日本の和には矛盾があります。

　欧米の人に「ハーモニー」の定義を尋ねると、たいていの場合、「グループの中のいろんな音／意見が、共通の目的に向かって一緒に演奏する／働くこと」のように返答します。ですから、彼らの和の定義には、意見の対立やそれに起因する居心地の悪さに対処しつつ、違う意見を交換する場を保つ包括性があるのです。

Attitude (Tone color)

The tolerance towards differences that I mentioned above is also an attitude. Another major difference in attitude between Japan and the Western world is about risk taking. This attitude is well expressed in Japanese language. We often say things like the following:

Common Japanese Expressions	Positeve Expressions
• Be careful not to get hurt!	• Good luck!
• We should take measures so that we won't lose money with this.	• We should optimize our investment results.
• We need to plan ahead so that our production won't be disrupted.	• We need to plan ahead so that we can sustain good production levels.

Overall, we are concerned about risks and want to take measures to avoid them. However, Westerners are willing to take risks for potential gain. Even when taking risks didn't create good results, the risk taker is not penalized very much or very long. Westerner's common sense is that you need to take risks in order to create something new, beneficial, or profitable. So, we need to reframe our wording with a more optimistic, risk-taking attitude.

Lastly, how can we express "I'm not good at speaking English" in a positive way?

態度——音色

　違いに対する寛容度は、態度の一つです。日本人と欧米人との間にある、もう一つの大きな態度の違いはリスクへの対応です。日本人のリスク回避の態度は、日本語によく表現されています。下は日本人がよく言うことと、それを前向きにした表現です。

日本人がよく使う表現	より前向きな表現
• 怪我しないように気をつけてね！	• 頑張って！
• この案件で損をしないように対応しよう。	• 投資効果の最適化が必要だ。
• 生産が滞らないよう、先々の計画を立てる必要がある。	• 生産レベルを維持するために、計画を立てる必要がある。

　概して、私たちはリスクを心配し、リスクを避ける方策を立てようとします。しかし欧米人は、何かを得る可能性にかけ、損するリスクを覚悟します。リスク負担がよい結果をもたらさなかったときでさえ、リスクを担った人は大したお咎めを受けず、受けたとしても短期間です。何か新しいものや、役に立つもの、利益を作り出すには、リスクの負担が必要だというのが、欧米人の常識です。ですから私たちは、より楽観的でリスクを覚悟する態度で言葉を選ばなければいけないのです。

　それでは最後に、「英語を話すのは苦手です」を前向きな表現にするとどうなるでしょう。

"I'm not good at speaking English"

⬇

"I'm developing my English conversation skills."

Some of you may think that this is not very useful. Although framing something positively doesn't improve the actual level of your English skills, you are able to demonstrate your positive attitude and give others a positive image of yourself. And that can have a positive impact on how effectively you can communicate, as well as on your relationship with others around the world.

■ 7 Elements [5]
Grammar (Form)

Most of us know enough English grammar. Some Japanese worry that they can't remember certain grammatical points that they learned in middle school or high school. But think about this: we all speak Japanese even though we don't remember Japanese grammar. If you are concerned about the grammar, read something that is written for middle school students. If you have a thick book on grammar, use it as a reference for specific questions instead of reading it like a book. What I recommend is to actually read English articles and learn how to say things. When I encounter an English sentence that requires a bit of mind-twisting, I try to memorize

「英語を話すのは苦手です」

⬇

「英会話力を伸ばす努力をしています。」

　こういった言葉の綾はあまり役に立たないと思われる人もいるでしょう。もちろん、何かを前向きに見ることが、あなたの英語能力の実際の改善につながるわけではありません。けれども、あなたの積極的な態度を示すことで、相手にあなたの前向きなイメージを与えることができます。そしてそれは、世界の人との人間関係だけでなく、コミュニケーションに確かな効果をもたらします。

■ 7つの要素 [5]
文法──形式

　私たちには英文法の知識は十分あります。中学や高校で学んだ文法を思い出せないと、心配する人がいます。けれども考えてみてください。私たちは日本語の文法を覚えてなくても、しゃべれます。もし英語の文法を気にされているなら、中学生向けに書かれたものを読んでください。分厚い文法書をお持ちなら、本のように最初から順番に読むのではなく、索引を使って必要なところだけを読んでみてください。私がおすすめしたいのは、英語で書かれた文章を読んで、実際に物事をどうやって伝えるのかを学ぶことです。直観的にわからない（だから、自分では書けそうにない）英語の文章に出会ったとき、私は文法を分析するのではなく、文章そのものを覚えるように心がけています。赤ちゃんが話すの

it, instead of analyzing it grammatically. That's how babies learn how to speak.

If you want to keep your non-Japanese audience engaged One of my clients that I met through Skype one evening answered this question, "How comfortable are you with English?" with the following sentence:

I feel comfortable using English even my English skills is not good like a baby.

This sentence isn't correct grammatically, however, most native speakers can understand what he wants to say. One of the things he and you can do is to make the sentence a bit shorter and correct the grammatical errors.

I feel comfortable using English. My English skills are not good. I speak like a baby.

Then, make the meaning clearer. Babies babble but don't speak. So, I'll change "a baby" to "a child."

I feel comfortable using English. However, my English is as good as a child's.

If you can, please add one more sentence. I always recommend that once you start talking (or writing), say/write at least three sentences.

I feel comfortable. But my English may sound like a child speaking. I learn English on the commuter train.

を学ぶのと同じ方法です。

✦ コミュニケーションの極意 3 ［3文話す（書く）］

　ある夜（日本の朝）にSkypeを通じて会ったクライアント
は、事前アンケートの中の「英語でコミュニケーションする快
適度は？」という質問に次のように答えていました。

I feel comfortable using English even my English skills is
not good like a baby.

　この英文は、文法的には正確ではありませんが、ネイティブ・
スピーカーのほとんどは、彼が言いたいことを理解できます。
彼と読者の皆さんができることの一つは、文を短くし、文法的
な間違いを正すことです。

I feel comfortable using English. My English skills are
not good. I speak like a baby.

　そして、意味がより明確になるようにします。赤ちゃんは、
「ばぁ」とか「ぶぅ」とか音を出しますが、言語を話しているわ
けではありません。ですから、赤ちゃんを子どもに変えます。

I feel comfortable using English. However, my English is
as good as a child's.

　できれば、文をもう一つ足してください。いったん話し始め
たら（もしくは書き始めたら）、最低でも3文話す（書く）こ
とを、常におすすめしています。

I feel comfortable. But my English may sound like a child
speaking. I learn English on the commuter train.

61

In the above example, you may feel that it's not sophisticated enough. However, you can clearly convey what you want to say, and the chance of misunderstanding is much lower. That is the most important point when you're communicating across cultures in a foreign language.

Finally, one last update to the response:

I feel comfortable. But I need to improve my English skills. I want to speak and write in English more clearly. So, I read an English article every morning on my way to work.

This response has a direct response (I feel comfortable), a "what" (I need to improve my English skills), a "why" (I want to speak and write in English more clearly), and an example of what you're doing to achieve this. This is clear and very positive.

■ 7 Elements [6]
Relationships (Texture)

This is about the overall quality of your communication. If the communication is two-way and you and your conversation partner(s) have exchanged information and opinions, then, it was a success in terms of communication quality, even if you still have some disagreements with them. To achieve this, you need to maintain openness, give others a fair chance to speak, and share your opinions clearly.

上記の例では、もしかするとあまり知的に響かないと感じる
かもしれません。しかし、言いたいことを明確に伝えているの
で、誤解が生じる可能性はぐっと減ります。それが外国語で文
化の違う人と話すときに一番大切なことです。

　最後にもう一つ、上の返答に変更を加えさせてください。

I feel comfortable. But I need to improve my English
skills. I want to speak and write in English more clearly.
So, I read an English article every morning on my way to
work.

　この例では、直接的な返答（苦痛なく話せる）と「何」（英
語のスキルを改善する必要がある）と「理由」（もっと明確な
英語を話したり書いたりしたい）、そしてそれを達成するため
に何をしているかが入っています。これは明確で非常に前向き
な返答です。

■ 7つの要素 [6]
関係——質感、旋律と和音による構成

　これは、あなたのコミュニケーションの全体的な出来栄えに関
することです。双方向のコミュニケーションができ、相手と情報
や意見の交換ができたのであれば、同意できない点が残っていて
も、そのコミュニケーションは成功です。これを達成するには、
常に人の意見を聞く用意があること、相手に話す機会を提供する
こと、そして自分の意見を明確に伝えることが必要です。

Japanese, including myself, tend to be disappointed when we learn there's a difference in our views or opinions, and we inadvertently show our disappointment on our faces or in the tone of voice or in our posture. We also tend to get discouraged by the differences, or judge others based on those differences. This is probably because Japan is a consensus-based society, and we're not accustomed to working with differences or negotiating regarding differences. So, we need to remind ourselves that we need to keep our minds open to new or different ideas. This takes some practice.

We also need to be cognizant of the goals that we seek in the long term. I've seen people who won an argument, but lost a relationship or lost someone's trust because of it.

■ 7 Elements [7]
Speaking slow or fast, volume and pitch (Dynamics)

Consider a person learning to play a piece of music on the piano. If he stops learning it when he becomes able to play it through, he'll miss the opportunity to become a good performer of that piece. That is only the beginning of the process of making good music. He needs to keep working on it so that he can express the composer's intentions. The same is true in communication. You may be able to speak English flawlessly in terms of grammar. However, if you can't get your points across, or if you don't convey your feelings—like your

私も含め日本人は、ものの見方や意見に違いがあると知ると
がっかりし、それが知らずしらず顔や声や姿勢にでてしまいがち
です。また、やる気をなくしたり、相手をその違いだけで否定的
に判断したりします。これはおそらく、日本がコンセンサスに基
づく社会で、違いを認めながら働いたり、また違いについて面と
向かって交渉することに慣れていないからです。ですから私たち
は、新しいまたは違うアイデアに対して常に聞く耳を持つよう、
自分に言い聞かせなければなりません。これには、練習が必要で
す。

　また、長期的に達成したい目標を常に意識する必要もありま
す。その時どきの議論で相手を打ち負かすことに一生懸命になり
すぎて、人間関係をダメにしてしまったり、信用をなくしてし
まった日本人を私は何度も見てきました。

■ 7つの要素 [7]

話す速度、声の音量と高低──ダイナミックス

　ピアノである曲を弾こうとしている人を考えてみましょう。も
しその人がその曲を最後まで通して弾けるようになったところ
で練習をやめたら、その曲の立派な演奏者になる機会を逃してし
まいます。そこからが、聞き応えのある演奏への道のりです。作
曲者の意図を表現できるよう、さらに練習しなければなりませ
ん。コミュニケーションについても同じことが言えます。もうあ
なたは、文法的に間違いのない英語を話せるかもしれません。し
かし、あなたの言いたいポイントを相手に伝えられなかったり、
善意や共通の目標に対するコミットメントなど、あなたの気持ち

good will and your commitment towards common goals—then the conversation may not be counted as a success. Like musicians who use speed and the volume of the sound to accentuate the mood of the music, we also need to use speed and volume to emphasize our points and our feelings.

In general, we need to pronounce verbs more clearly, and with strength. When speaking in Japanese, the verb comes at the end of the sentence, and most Japanese can read your mind through context (who, where, when, and how), so we don't have to make our point (what) very clear. However, in English, you need to say your point first, and you need to speak clearly and sometimes a bit more slowly to emphasize the verb.

Also, when we know there's a disagreement, we tend to speak rather quietly without sustained eye contact. This can create an unintended result: you appear to be less confident about your opinion, and you may appear to be accepting their opinion. And later, when they learn that you are not in agreement with them, they may feel as if they have been tricked. So, we need to convey our positive attitude (I don't agree with your opinion, but I like working with you), and clearly convey our thoughts and feelings through dynamics as well as words.

Pronunciations

Having lived in the U.S. for more than twenty-seven years,

を伝えられなかったとしたら、コミュニケーションが成功したとは言えません。演奏の速度と音量を使って曲のムードを強調する演奏者のように、私たちも話す速度や声の音量、高低を使って、伝えたいポイントや気持ちを強調しなければなりません。

　一般に、日本人は動詞をもっとはっきり、強く発音すべきです。日本語では、動詞は文の一番最後にきます。また、日本人はたいていコンテキスト（誰とどこで、いつ、どのようにしてなどの情報）を通じて、相手の気持ちや考えを推測することができます。ですから、日本人どうしで話すとき、ポイント（何）を明確にする必要があまりありません。しかし、英語で話すときは、自分の言いたいポイントを真っ先に述べ、また、動詞を強調するために、明確に、ときにはゆっくりめに話す必要があるのです。

　また、日本人は意見に相違があるとわかっていると、相手の目を見ずに、静かめに話してしまいがちです。これは、意図しない結果をもたらしかねません。自分の意見に自信がなく、相手の意見を受け入れたという印象を与えてしまうからです。あとで、実はあなたが同意していないことがわかると、相手はだまされたと感じてしまうこともあります。ですから、前向きな態度（あなたの意見には同意できないけれども、あなたと働くのは好きだ）を伝えつつ、自分の考えや気持ちを言葉だけでなく、声の高低を使って伝える必要があるのです。

発音

　アメリカに27年以上住んだ今、アメリカのテレビ番組と映画を

I mostly watch American TV programs and American movies. So, when I see Japanese TV programs, I sometimes don't understand a word, and need to play the same part over and over. This is because I am now so used to hearing consonants pronounced clearly in English. Japanese sounds that include consonants like K, S, and T are hard to hear when pronounced softly. So, I imagine native speakers of English may have a similar problem with our Japanese English.

When I worked at a consulting firm in New York City, I went to the cafeteria and ordered the same sandwich for lunch for two weeks before I moved on to a different lunch item. The person who was behind the tall glass deli counter couldn't understand me as I said "chicken on a roll." Sometimes the person ahead of me ordered the same "chicken on a roll." Although I couldn't hear the difference between his pronunciation and mine, the deli person had no difficulty understanding his order. After a while, they figured out that I would always order the same thing. So, to this date, I don't know if my pronunciation improved, or if he started to humor me.

I think the problem was three-fold. First, my voice is naturally low, so I needed to raise the pitch a bit, so that the deli person could hear me in the noisy place. Second, I needed to speak louder so that my voice could carry over the big glass cover that was as tall as me. But the third and most important was that I needed to pronounce the consonants clearly: the "chi" sound of chicken, and the "r" sound of roll. He might

見ることが断然多くなりました。日本のテレビ番組を見ると、ときどき聞き取れない言葉があり、何度も戻して聞き直します。これは、私が英語ではっきりと発音される子音に慣れてしまったせいです。日本語のか行、さ行、た行の子音は、弱く発音されると聞きにくいのです。ですから、ネイティブ・スピーカーが日本人の英語を聞くと、同じような問題を経験するのだと思います。

　ニューヨーク市のコンサルティング会社で働いていたとき、ランチにカフェテリアに行って、同じものを2週間注文し続けました。高いガラス張りのカウンターの向こうにいる人は、私の"Chicken on a roll.（丸いパンにチキンを挟んだサンドイッチ）"の注文をわかってくれません。ときどき、前に並んでいる人が同じものを注文します。私には、その人と私の発音との違いが聞き取れませんでしたが、デリの人はその人の注文はちゃんとわかるのです。しばらくすると、私がいつも同じものを注文するとばれてしまいました。ですから、今でも私の発音がよくなったのか、それともただ調子を合わせてくれたのかはわかりません。

　私の英語の問題は三つあったと思います。まず、私の声は生まれつき低いので、ざわざわとうるさいデリの中で聞こえるよう、音程を少し高めにする必要がありました。次に、私の背と同じくらいの高さのガラス越しに私の声がデリの人に届くよう、音量を上げるべきでした。しかし、最も重要なのは、子音をきちんと発音すべきだったことです。チキンの"chi"の音、ロールの"r"の音です。デリの人にはきっと、"icken on a oll"と聞こえてしまい、

have heard my order as "icken on a oll" and that didn't make sense to him at all.

So, for Japanese, speaking English requires cultural shifts, musical elements expressed in different ways, and different sets of pronunciations. No wonder it is so hard! I hope you'll read the following chapters and gather some insights on how to improve your English.

❖ Summary ❖

Speaking in English means that you not only translate your Japanese into English but you also adapt to English culture: the ways of expressing things in English and behavioral patterns.

You need to change your perception and communication modes from the analogue to digital mode.

It is also important that you don't limit yourself to your group's consensus, and clearly define your own ideas and opinions. Especially in the Western world, people build connections based on individuals. Therefore, being able to express your own perspective is the keys to cultivating relationships through English communication.

何のことかさっぱりわからなかったのだと思います。

　日本人が通じる英語を話すには、文化のシフトと、英語と日本語の音楽的要素の使い方の違い、そして、違った発音のしかたを習得する必要があります。どうりで、英語を話すのが難しいワケです！ 以下の章が、あなたの英語上達のヒントになることを願います。

❖ まとめ ❖

　英語で話すということは、頭の中で日本語を英語に置き換えるだけでなく、英語文化の中での表現方法や行動様式に適応することでもある。

　英語で話すとき、知覚モードとコミュニケーション・モードをデジタルに切り替える必要がある。

　グループのコンセンサスから離れて、自分なりの考えを明確にすることも大事。特に欧米社会での人と人のつながりは個人ベースなので、自分の考え方を知り、表現できるようにすることが、英語での人間関係作りには非常に大切。

Let's try the following:

· Write your opinions in English. This can provide a great opportunity of your self-discovery.

· Try to remember situations where you responded by saying "I'm not sure" or "I'll check and get back to you," and create your responses in the digital mode.

· Pick a few elements of English that seem easier for you to adapt or that you're interested in, and apply a new way of speaking English. Reading English articles emphasizing these elements is also useful.

やってみよう

・自分なりの意見を英語で書いてみる。面白い自己発見のきっかけになるかも。

・過去に「はっきりわかりません」「確認して、連絡します」と対応した状況を思い出し、自分の考えをデジタル・モードで書いてみる。

・前出の英語の７つの要素のうち、取り組みやすいものや興味のあるものに挑戦してみる。英語の文章をこれらの要素を強調しながら読むのも一つの方法。

Chapter II
How to Communicate Positively

The sun helps me be physically active and feel positive about life. The shorter days of autumn in the American Northeast makes me feel tired for no reason and overwhelmed by a workload that I know can actually be finished easily. I casually mentioned this to my friends at our morning coffee get-together. Several days later, one of them showed up at my house with a book, A Daybook of Positive Thinking. On the first page, it says, "Be Positive … Be Happy," which ironically depressed me even more, because it didn't give me any tools that I could use. When the sky is grey, there's no use in making believe that it's blue. The positive part of this experience was not the book, but my friend's act of kindness, which was a wonderful surprise. I feel lucky to have good friends like her.

In this chapter, I'd like to talk about active communication, which is speaking, as opposed to passive communication, or listening. I'd like to provide tools that you can use in order to

第2章
プラス志向のコミュニケーション

　太陽の光があると、体を動かしたくなり、気分も明るくなります。秋になって、アメリカ北東部で日照時間が短くなると、理由もなく疲れてしまったり、簡単にできるとわかっている仕事で気持ちが押しつぶされてしまったりします。朝のコーヒーの集まりで、何気なくこのことを口にしました。すると数日後、友だちの一人が「ポジティブ思考の日誌」という本を届けてくれました。本を開くと最初のページに「ポジティブになれ……幸せになれ」とあり、皮肉にも私はもっと憂うつになってしまいました。ポジティブに、そしてハッピーになるための方法が書かれていなかったからです。空が灰色のときに、青い空が広がっているフリをしても助けになりません。この一件のポジティブな部分は本の内容ではなく、うれしくもあり、びっくりもした友だちの親切さでした。彼女のようなよい友だちに恵まれ、本当にありがたいです。

　この章では、積極的なコミュニケーション（受け身の、聞くコミュニケーションではなく）、つまり「話すこと」について述べます。よい結果を出すためのツールを提供したいと思います。ご存

create positive results. You may not know this, but few Japanese enjoy a reputation of being a positive communicator in English.

What is "positive" in communication?

Just as in the story of "The Emperor's New Clothes," it is sometimes counter-productive and self-defeating to pretend that you have something that you actually don't, or to say something you don't actually believe in, in order to get along with others. Although a positive attitude can certainly help you with difficult situations, attitude alone rarely makes a real difference.

The "positive" communication that I'd like to talk about is the communication that increases your understanding of your conversation partners as well as their understanding of you. Some Japanese become overly friendly and very agreeable in English communication, but if their friendly communication style doesn't help them or their speaking partners understand one another, then they might feel empty after the conversation, like the emperor wearing invisible clothes.

So, I'd like to share some useful tools that you can use to describe your situations, ideas, opinions, and feelings, so that you can tell your conversation partners what you're thinking and feeling.

There are situations where I know my American friends and I are talking about the same opinions or feelings, but they and

じないかもしれませんが、英語のポジティブなコミュニケーターだという評判を得ている日本人は、ほとんどいないのです。

コミュニケーションで「ポジティブ」とは？

「裸の王さま」の話にもあるように、相手と調子を合わせるために、ないものを持っているフリをしたり、信じてもいないことを言ったりしても、よい結果は出ませんし、目的達成のチャンスを自ら潰すようなものです。前向きな姿勢は、難しい状況の中で助けになることはありますが、姿勢だけで本当の成果を出せることはほとんどありません。

ここで検討したい「ポジティブな」コミュニケーションとは、あなたと対話相手が、お互いの理解を深められるコミュニケーションです。英語で話すとき、親しみやすさを過度に強調したり、相手にすぐ同調したがる人がいますが、親交的なコミュニケーション・スタイルがお互いの理解につながらなければ、見えない洋服を着た王さまのように、対話の後に虚しさを感じるかもしれません。

ですから、あなたの考えと気持ちをきちんと相手に伝えられるよう、あなたの状況やアイデア、意見、気持ちをあるがままに述べるツールを紹介したいと思います。

アメリカ人の友人と話していて、まったく同じ意見や気持ちでも、違う表現を使っていることがあります。たとえば、私なら「気

I express the same thing in different ways. For example, at a time where I would say, "Be careful!" my American friends may say, "Good luck!" or "Enjoy!" Looking at a glass of water, I may describe it as "half empty," but Americans may describe the same glass as "half full." This is a difference in perception and attitude (how you look at it), but also how Japanese and others describe things in their native language. In other words, if we translate our Japanese response into English word for word, it might come across as odd or negative to native speakers of English. This is more about culture than language. That is why this is tricky.

◆ Path to Mastery 4

- Communicate in ways that make our conversation partners interested in what we say

- Create more opportunities to be with our conversation partners (setting up the next get-together or meeting)

- Make the best use of opportunities to exchange ideas, opinions, and feelings

- Try to ensure that both parties get something they want, such as information, a compromise, a shared goal, or positive feelings about each other

- Always try to create pathways for better relationships

"Positive communication" is communication that increases

をつけてね」という場面で、アメリカ人の友だちは「頑張って！」「楽しんでね！」と声をかけます。水の入ったコップを見て、私が「半分しかない」と描写するところで、彼らは「半分もある」と評価します。これは、認識と姿勢（物事をどう見るか）の違いですが、日本人と海外の人がそれぞれの母国語でどう話すかにも左右されます。つまり、私たちの状況に対する日本語の反応をそのまま英語に訳して伝えると、奇妙に聞こえたり否定的に聞こえたりします。これは言語の問題というより文化の問題で、だからこそややこしいのです。

◆ コミュニケーションの極意 4　［理解を深める］

- 私たちが言うことに相手が興味をもてるようなコミュニケーションのしかたをする

- 相手と直接会って話す機会を作る（一緒に何かを楽しむ機会、またはミーティングを設定する）

- アイデアや意見、気持ちを伝えあう機会を最大限に利用する

- それぞれが望んでいるものを何か得られるようにする。たとえば、情報や妥協、共通の目標、相手に対する好意的な気持ちなど

- よりよい人間関係につながる道筋を作り続ける

「プラス志向のコミュニケーション」とは、お互いをより広くま

or deepens one another's understanding. That will enable you and your conversation partner to create and cultivate good relationships.

In Chapter I, we discussed three categories that can make communication in English challenging for Japanese:

Listening culture vs. speaking culture

Group-oriented culture vs. individualistic culture

Analogue vs. digital modes of communication

In this chapter, I'll focus on speaking as an individual, and how to shift your analogue mode of communication to the digital mode. These three aspects (speaking culture, individualistic culture, and digital mode) are interrelated and interwoven. So, if you improve one of these aspects, you may also be able to improve the other aspects of your communication.

Being honest is the best strategy when it comes to your level of understanding

I'm not a shy person, and I can ask questions and don't mind if others laugh at me. But when I was struggling with English, for the first three years in the U.S., I said "yes" more often than I should have. When someone explained something to me, and I didn't understand everything but felt that I got the gist of it,

た深く理解できるコミュニケーションです。それにより、よい人間関係を築き、さらに深めることができます。

　第1章で、英語のコミュニケーションを難しくしているものを三つ検討しました。

　　聞く文化と話す文化
　　グループを大切にする文化と個人を大切にする文化
　　アナログ・モードとデジタル・モードのコミュニケーション

　この章では、個人として話すこと、そしてどうやってアナログ・モードをデジタル・モードに変換するかについて話します。これらの三つの特徴（話す文化と個人を大切にする文化、デジタル・モード）はお互いに関連し絡み合っています。ですから、どれか一つを改善すると、残り二つの改善にもつながります。

理解度に関しては、正直であることが最善策

　私ははにかみ屋ではありませんし、質問をして他人に笑われても気にするたちではありません。けれども、まだ英語に自信のなかったアメリカでの最初の3年間は、必要以上に「yes」と返事をしました。誰かが何かを説明してくれたとき、完全に理解できなかったけれども要点はとらえたと感じると、「yes」と答えまし

I would say "yes." I thought "Well, I can try first and then ask questions if I come across something that I don't understand." I'm not alone in this: many Japanese (and other Asians) tend to avoid saying "no" in these situations because in Japanese communication, the burden is usually on the listener; if the listener didn't understand something, the listener would be responsible for his/her lack of understanding. This is possible in Japan because we usually share context with each other, and can understand or at least make a good guess regarding the speaker's true intentions. Also, we feel bad or impolite to ask questions after an expert on a subject or a person with authority has explained something to us, due to our sense of hierarchy.

Although it is natural for Japanese to choose vagueness or uncertainly rather than saying, "I don't understand" bluntly (in the Japanese sense), non-Japanese would neither understand nor appreciate our cultural reasons for why we can't allow ourselves to say, "Sorry, I don't understand," or "No, I don't quite get it." So, we need to switch our Japanese mode of "being polite" to the clear-cut, yes/no mode (this is the digital mode).

My approach based on my Japanese politeness usually didn't produce good results in work and in relationships with my co-workers. I know from my experiences that saying, "I don't understand," is even tougher after I requested the same explanation for the second time. When he or she finished

た。「まずやってみて、わからないことが出てきたら、また聞けば
いい」と思っていたのです。このように対応するのは、私だけで
はありません。日本人（そしてアジア人）の多くは、このような状
況で"no"というのを避けがちです。なぜなら、日本人どうしのコ
ミュニケーションでは、通常、理解するのは「聞き手」の仕事だか
らです。もし、聞き手が理解できなければ、理解できなかった責
任を負うのは聞き手というわけです。これが可能なのは、日本で
はお互いの状況を共有するので、話している人の真の意図を理解
できるか、だいたい予測できるからです。また上下関係を気にす
るため、専門知識のある人や権限のある人が何かを説明してくれ
た後に質問することが、居心地悪かったり、失礼だと感じます。

　ぶっきらぼうに「わかりません」と言うより、あいまいなままに
したり、不確かなままにしておくのは、日本人にとっては自然で
す。しかし海外の人は、日本人が「すみません、わかりません」と
か「内容がよく理解できません」と言えない文化的な理由を理解
できませんし、好意的に見ることもできません。ですから、私た
ちは英語で話すときは「あいまいで丁寧な」モードから明快な「イ
エス／ノー」モード（デジタル・モード）に切り替える必要があり
ます。
　日本の礼儀を基本とする私の物事の進め方では、アメリカでの
仕事や人間関係であまりよい結果を得られませんでした。一度な
らず、同じ説明を二度してもらった後に「わかりません」というの
は、もっと辛いものです。それで、「わかった？」とか「内容の筋
を追えましたか？」と聞かれると、ついパブロフの犬の条件反射

explaining and asked me, "Do you understand me?" or "Do you follow me?" I would say "Yes," like a dog involved in Pavlov's experiments on reflexes.

Let's think about some possible scenarios at work where I didn't say, "I don't understand." If my co-workers later learn that I actually didn't understand, then they may feel that I was not being honest or, even worse, that I betrayed them. They may also be very upset because I wasted their time. These negative feelings may increase even further, if he or she didn't find out about my lack of understanding until much later, say for example, three weeks later. It would then be a rude awakening that my work doesn't align with their expectations or the direction that they thought I had agreed upon. This could harm my relationship with them.

So, please avoid making the same mistake I made. By saying, "I don't understand," when I don't, my colleagues can at least understand that I don't have a full grasp of the subject matter. This is the minimum understanding that you and your business/conversation partners can share.

So, what is a more positive approach when you think you understand 80 percent but are not sure about the rest? I recommend that you state what you understand, and then ask questions regarding the part you are not sure about.

のように「はい」と答えてしまいました。

　わからなかったのに「わかりません」と言えなかった場合にど
んなことが起きるか、考えてみましょう。後でアメリカ人の同僚
が、実は私が理解していなかったということを知ると、私が正直
でなかったと思うか、悪くすると、騙されたと感じるかもしれま
せん。時間を無駄にされたと感じて、ムッとするかもしれません。
もしずっと後、たとえば３週間後まで、私が理解しなかったこと
を相手が知らずにいると、私に対する悪い感情はさらに増大する
でしょう。そして、私のやった作業が彼らの期待にそぐわないか、
もしくは同意したはずの方向性と一致しないと、非常に不愉快な
思いをすることになります。これは、彼らとの関係を悪化させま
す。
　ですから、皆さんは私と同じ間違いをしないでください。わか
らないときに「わからない」と言うことで、案件に関する私の理解
が十分でないということを、相手にわかってもらえます。これは
あなたと、仕事や対話の相手が共有できる、最低限の理解なので
す。
　では、理解度が80パーセントで、残りについては自信がない
とき、どんな風に対応するのがプラス志向なのでしょうか？　私が
おすすめしたいのは、まず何がわかったかを伝えた後に、不安な
点について質問することです。

"I understand that the deadline for my task is next Friday, and that I should complete the research on the warehouse's readiness for the new delivery system. How would you recommend we measure their readiness?"

"I think I understand the action items; however, I have a couple of questions. First ..."

"I didn't quite understand the logic when you explained how we are revamping the customer service. Can you explain it again?"

"I think I'm on the same page with you, but would like to clarify a couple of points."

"I understand the overall strategy. But what kind of changes should I make? What is required in order for us to succeed?"

"I understand all the necessary steps that we need to take. But what are we trying to achieve by this? Can you explain the reasons behind this again?"

Asking questions can clarify where you are having difficulty, and that'll help others explain the subject with a specific focus. Asking questions can also become the process to shift analogue information to digital information. Let's say you have a general idea of what you need to do, but if you can't list concrete items to tackle or next steps in your head, then you need to ask questions.

「作業の締め切りは来週の金曜日だとわかっていますし、倉庫が新しい配送システムに対応する準備ができているかどうかについて、調査を完了しないければならないこともわかっています。準備の状況を判断するおすすめの方法はありますか？」

「作業項目については、理解できていると思います。しかし、二つほど質問があります。まず最初に……」

「顧客サービスの改善方法について説明されたとき、その論理がよく理解できませんでした。もう一度説明してもらえますか？」

「あなたと同じ理解だと思うのですが、明確にしたい点が二つあります」

「全体的な戦略は理解できました。しかし、どのような変更をすればよいのでしょう？　私たちが成功するためには何が必要ですか？」

「今後とるべきステップについては理解できました。しかし、これによってどんなことが達成できるのでしょう？　理由をもう一度説明してもらえますか？」

　質問をすることで、あなたがどこでつまずいているのかを伝えることができ、相手は的確な説明をしやすくなります。質問をすることは、アナログからデジタル情報への変換です。たとえば、何をしなければならないかについて、だいたいの理解があったとします。けれども、具体的な作業や段取りのリストが頭に浮かばなければ、質問をすべきです。

One of my Chinese clients told me that he'll make sure that both parties agree on at least one thing: what the next step is. When people can't agree on anything after a discussion, he'll ask, "What is our next step?" repeatedly until he gets something out of that meeting. It may not work every time, but creating a sense of "we're moving forward" is a positive thing. Nobody wants to conclude a meeting without a positive outcome.

Path to Mastery 6

I also strongly recommend that you summarize the meeting at the end, or approximately every thirty minutes if it's a long meeting. You can say something like the following:

"Let me summarize what we have discussed so far."

"Let me confirm a couple of points."

"Excuse me, can I see if my understanding is the same as yours?"

"I just want to see if my understanding is aligned with the overall direction."

"Sorry, I'm not sure that I have everything straight in my head. I'd like to clarify a couple of points here."

私のある中国人のクライアントは、最低でも両者が一つのことについて合意するようにしているそうです。それは、次のステップは何かということです。話し合っても何も合意できなかった場合、彼は必ず「次のステップは何か？」という質問をくり返し、ミーティングの最後に何等かの成果が得られるようにします。いつもこの手でうまくいくとは限りませんが、「ともに前進している」という雰囲気を作るのは、プラス志向の行動です。前向きな結果がないまま、ミーティングを終えたい人はいませんから。

コミュニケーションの極意6 [内容の要約をこまめにやる]

　ぜひおすすめしたいのは、ミーティングの最後に、長いミーティングであれば30分ごとに、あなたがミーティングの内容を要約して確認することです。以下のようなフレーズを使うといいでしょう。

　「ここまでの討議内容を要約させてください」

　「ポイントを二つ確認させてください」

　「すみませんが、私の理解があなたのと同じかどうか確認させてください」

　「私の理解が全体的な方向性に沿っているかどうか確認したいのです」

　「すみません。すべてをきちんと理解できているかどうか心もとないので、二つほど確認させてください」

Keep talking positively

I strongly recommend that once you start talking, you continue for at least three sentences. I'll insist on this point throughout this book. The reason is that whenever I tell native speakers of English that I encourage Japanese to complete at least three sentences, they get excited and say, "That's it! I never figured it out, but now I know why I feel get stuck when I speak with Japanese." They want to get to know you, but they are not getting enough information from you, so they don't know how to continue the conversation with you.

This issue is also cultural. Japanese are used to the pattern of "one answer for one question." On the other hand, native speakers are used to giving longer answers so that they can fully explain their perspective, theory, or idea to you. In their culture, the speaker is responsible for the success or the failure of communication. Therefore, figuratively and literally, we need to expand our explanation from one sentence to three sentences. In other words, we need to take more advantage of the opportunity to speak, and make sure we give clear answers to their questions.

When you speak long enough, you tend to reveal more about your opinions, feelings, or situations to your conversation partners, and that'll give them something to react to.

With my Japanese clients, I conduct an exercise that has

積極的に話し続ける

　ぜひ実行していただきたいのは、いったん話し始めたら、少なくとも3文は話し続けることです。この点については、この本の中で一貫してお願いし続けます。というのは、私がいつも日本人に対して最低でも3文は話すように勧めていることをネイティブ・スピーカーに伝えると、「それだ！ 今までわからなかったけど、どうして日本人と話すと話が進まないのかわかったよ！」と非常に喜んでくれるのです。彼らはあなたのことを知りたいのです。けれども十分な情報を会話の中で得られないので、どうやって会話を続ければいいのかわからないのです。

　この現象にも文化が影響しています。日本人は、「一問一答」のパターンに慣れています。一方、ネイティブ・スピーカーは長めの返答をして、自分の見方や理論、アイデアを十分に説明することに慣れています。彼らの文化では、コミュニケーションの成否の鍵を握っているのは、「話し手」なのです。ですから、私たちは説明を1文から3文に展開する必要があるのです。つまり、話す機会をもっとうまく利用するとともに、相手の質問に対して明確な返答をするようにします。

　長めに話すと、自然と自分の意見や気持ち、状況を相手に伝えることになり、相手はそれに反応することができます。

　これをわかっていただくために、私は日本人のクライアントに

two requirements. First, simple "yes" or "no" answers are not acceptable, as such answers will end the conversation right there. Second, they need to speak for at least three sentences. Then I ask a simple question like, "Do you like Mexican food?" I'm always interested in their reaction, because Mexican food isn't overly popular in Japan yet. Some say "Mmm …" or "Mexican food …" Since I won't respond to such a short statement, most of them realize after a few seconds that they have to keep talking. They then say something like, "I don't eat Mexican food." It takes a while until I hear three full sentences from them. We need to practice and get used to this.

In Japan, we are taught to be sure before we speak, and therefore, being spontaneous isn't our strong suit, and yet we need to respond to whatever topics comes up in conversations in English. This is quite a challenge.

◆ Path to Mastery 7

One tactic that I used when I was new to America was the following:

a. First, state a fact or something obvious

b. Then, give my own reaction to my first sentence

c. And finally, ask questions

[Example 1]

a. Mexican food is spicy.

b. I sweat when I eat spicy food.

二つの要件を満たすようにお願いして、対話の練習をします。一つ目の要件は、簡単な "yes" か "no" の答えはダメだということ。そのような返答では、会話がそこで途切れてしまうからです。二つ目は、必ず3文話すことです。そこまで説明して、「メキシコ料理はお好きですか？」といった簡単な質問をします。メキシコ料理はまだ日本では一般化していないので、クライアントの反応が楽しみです。「ん～」とか「メキシコ料理ねぇ……」と言う人もいます。そのような短い文に私は反応しませんから、数秒もするとほとんどの人は話し続けなければいけないことに気づきます。そのあと、「メキシコ料理は食べないです」などと言い、それから3文話し終わるまでしばらくかかります。練習をして、3文話すことに慣れましょう。

　日本では、内容が確実になってから話すように教えられますので、その場ですぐに反応するのは苦手です。ところが英語の対話では、どんな話題にもすぐに対応しなければなりません。これはなかなか大変です。

◆ コミュニケーションの極意 7 ［長く話す］

　アメリカに来たばかりのころ、私は次の手法を使いました。

　（手法1）　a. まず明らかな事実を述べ
　　　　　　　b. 自分の言ったことに対して反応し
　　　　　　　c. 最後に質問する

　［例1］
　　a. メキシコ料理はスパイスがきいています。
　　b. 辛い料理を食べると、汗がでます。

   c. Can I ask them to make the food less spicy at
      Mexican restaurants?

[Example 2]
  a. I had Mexican food in Tokyo once.

  b. It was expensive.

  c. Is Mexican food in the U.S. also expensive?

Another tactic that I used is:

a. State a fact

b. Then share what I know

c. And finally ask him/her if they're interested

[Example 3]
  a. I like Mexican food.

  b. I know a good restaurant near the train station.

  c. Can I ask them to make the food less spicy at
     Mexican restaurants?

Occasionally I receive negative reactions to the Mexican food question from Japanese.

- I'm not interested.
- I don't like it.
- I have nothing to say about it.
- I don't want to talk about it.
- Let's talk about something else.

I understand that they're just being honest. But being honest, in this case, doesn't create a positive result. These are abrupt and can sound like a rejection to the

c. メキシコ料理店で、あまり辛くしないように頼めますか？

[例2]
a. 東京で一度メキシコ料理を食べたことがあります。
b. けっこうな値段でした。
c. アメリカのメキシコ料理も高いですか？

もう一つの手法は、

（手法2）　a. 事実を述べ
　　　　　b. 知っている関連情報を伝えて
　　　　　c. 興味があるかどうかを相手に聞く

[例3]
a. 私はメキシコ料理が好きです。
b. 駅の近くのいいレストランを知っています。
c. 今度そこで一緒にランチをしませんか？

たまにですが、メキシコ料理の質問に否定的な返答をされることがあります。

・興味ないです。
・好きじゃないです。
・何も言うことはありません。
・それについて話したくありません。
・他のことを話しましょう。

　正直に話してくれただけだ、というのは承知しています。しかし残念ながら、この場合は正直なだけではよい結果がでません。こういった応答はぶっきらぼうで、対話自体を、もしくは対話の相手を拒否しているように響いてしまいます。まったく

conversation or to the person you're speaking with. It's not positive at all. So instead of a short, negative response, you can keep a friendly attitude and guide the conversation in the direction you want it to go.

[Example 4]
Sorry, but I'm not really interested in Mexican food. I love Chinese food, though. I'm very happy that there are many Chinese restaurants in the U.S.

[Example 5]
I'm not a big fan of Mexican food. I like Italian food the best. You know, something interesting is that one of my Italian friends doesn't like Italian food. He likes Japanese food. Isn't that funny?

[Example 6]
I'm not a foodie. I like simple meals like sandwiches and pizzas. I'm perfectly happy having a pizza and a beer and watching a baseball game on TV.

[Example 7]
I know this may sound boring, but I like Japanese food the best. Noodles, sushi, okonomiyaki. Would you like to try some Japanese food with me?

How to digitize your analogue information

Let me explain about analogue and digital modes of communication again. In the recipe for "Melted-Pepper

ポジティブではありません。ですから短い否定的な返答をするのではなく、友好的な態度を保ちつつ、対話を自分の好きな方向へ誘導しましょう。

[例4]
すみませんが、メキシコ料理にはあまり興味がありません。でも中国料理は大好きです。アメリカに中華料理店がたくさんあるので、うれしいです。

[例5]
メキシコ料理は苦手です。一番好きなのは、イタリア料理です。面白いのはですね、私のイタリア人の友だちはイタリア料理が嫌いで、日本料理が好きなんです。面白いでしょ？

[例6]
私はグルメじゃないんです。サンドイッチとかピザとかの簡単な食事が好きです。テレビで野球の試合を見ながらピザを食べてビールを飲めば、それでとっても幸せです。

[例7]
つまらないと思われるかもしれませんが、私は日本料理が一番好きです。麺類とか、お寿司、お好み焼き。一緒に日本料理を食べに行きませんか？

アナログ情報のデジタル化

　もう一度、コミュニケーションのアナログとデジタル・モードを説明します。「溶けた赤ピーマンのスプレッド」のレシピ

Spread" (published in the New York Times Magazine), there's a step described as below:

> After 5 minutes or so, or when the sound has turned from a steamy bubble to a more crackling sizzle, you'll want to stir about 30 seconds to a minute, to find any pieces that have caramelized, and make sure that they dissolve.

I know that chefs don't go by digital instructions. They use analogue information such as sound and smell and the look of the food in a pan, and adjust the heat, amount of liquid and the spices accordingly. But I'm not a chef, so I need digital instructions. I'll be completely lost if the recipe only gives me an analogue instruction like "when the sound has turned from a steamy bubble to a more crackling sizzle." Thank goodness, it also gives me the specific length of "5 minutes" so even I can cook and enjoy decent melted-pepper spread on sliced bread and drink wine with it.

Japanese culture is full of analogue information. According to Gomi Taro's Japanese Onomatopoeic Dictionary, Japanese language has three to five times more onomatopoetic words than English and other European languages. *Jiri jiri* is one of the 182 examples in the book, and has five different meanings.

1. Describes someone running out of patience and fretting
2. Describes something that draws closer little by little
3. Describes the scorching sun

（ニューヨーク・タイムズ・マガジン）に以下の記述があります。

「約5分後、もしくは音が水気の多い泡の音からパチパチという弾く音になったら、30秒から1分ほど炒め、甘味で焦げ目がついたところがあれば、それをほぐします」

プロのシェフは、デジタルな情報だけに頼って料理をしません。音や香りやフライパンの中の状況などのアナログ情報を使って、火を加減したり、水分やスパイスの量を調節します。でも私はシェフではないので、デジタルな情報が必要です。レシピの手順が「音がぐつぐつという泡の音から、パチパチという弾く音になったら」というアナログ情報だけだったら、途方に暮れてしまいます。ありがたいことに、このレシピは「5分」という明確な時間を教えてくれるので、私でもまぁまぁの溶けた赤ピーマン・スプレッドをパンにのせて、ワインと一緒に楽しむところにたどり着けます。

日本文化はアナログ情報が満載です。五味太郎著「日本語擬態語辞典」によると、英語やその他のヨーロッパ系言語に比べ、日本語には3倍から5倍の擬態語があるそうです。この本の182の擬態語の一つ「じりじり」には、5つの意味が挙げられています。

　1. 待ち切れず、じれる様子

　2. 少しずつ、迫るように進む様子

　3. 直射日光が照りつけるさま

4. Describes something that has been burned

5. Describes the sound of an alarm bell

Japanese have no problem determining the correct meaning of *jiri jiri* according to the situation; however, we need to explain what *jiri jiri* means to non-Japanese in each case so that they can have a better understanding of what we're talking about. When you do this, you're translating analogue information to digital information.

When I have a business session via Skype with people in Japan, I receive their questionnaire responses beforehand. One of the first questions is "How comfortable are you with English?" They usually write something like, "Not very," "Beginner level," "Basic conversation level," or "Can't speak." So, I ask them at the start of my session, "How would you evaluate your English on a scale of one to ten? Ten means you can do your job well with your English. You don't have to speak it fluently. If you can get things done in English, you can give yourself ten." Most of them rate themselves in the range of two to four. Then, I ask them what kinds of skills are included in their score. Even when if they rate themselves at a one, they are still doing something well. What I do with this process is to convert "analogue information," which is based on "feelings" to "digital information," which is based on "facts and an analysis of them." For example, "I can greet others and say what I need to say, but I can't express myself well enough

4. 焼け焦げるさま

　5. ベルなどが鳴る音

　状況に照らし合わせて、日本人は「じりじり」の意味するところ
を正確に判断できます。しかし海外の人に対しては、私たちが何
を表現しようとしているのかを理解してもらうために、それぞれ
の状況における「じりじり」の意味を説明しなければなりません。
この作業をするとき、あなたはアナログ情報をデジタル情報に翻
訳していることになります。

　日本にいる人とスカイプを通じてビジネスのセッションをす
るとき、事前にクライアントのアンケートを受け取ります。最初
の質問の一つは、「英語でコミュニケーションする快適度は？」で
す。ほとんどのクライアントが、「あまり」「初心者程度」「基本
的な会話レベル」「話せません」などと書いてきます。そこでセッ
ションの初めに、こう質問します。「あなたの英語を1から10の
目盛りで評価するとしたら、いくつになりますか？ 流暢な英語を
話す必要はありません。英語で充分仕事ができるのであれば、10
にしてください」すると、ほとんどの人が2から4と答えます。次
に、その評価の中に英語のどんなスキルが含まれているかを聞き
ます。仮に「1」と答えたとしても、何かをうまくやっているので
す。この過程の中で私がやろうとしているのは、「感覚」に基づい
たアナログ情報から「事実とその分析」に基づいたデジタル情報
への変換です。たとえば、「挨拶はできますし、必要なことは伝
えられますが、表現がまだ未熟で、自分のことを相手にわかって
もらえません」という方がずっと具体的です。相手に具体的な情
報を提供し、また、あなたの質問に対して明確な返事をもらえる

to make others understand me," is much more concrete. I hope you'll use this "analogue to digital" process to prepare statements and questions in advance of meetings with other English speakers so that you can give them more concrete information and receive clear answers to your questions.

We have images in our minds, but sometimes interpreting those images into words that describe facts, ideas, and concrete behaviors isn't easy. I'm not saying that images are not useful—on the contrary! Images can be very useful if we can communicate the content of the image clearly to others.

And it is not that non-Japanese always talk in the digital mode. For example, American parents often say to their kids, "I want you to be happy." But what "happy" means can be very different from one person to another. For some, it may be about spending their free time doing something fun, and for other people, it may be about contributing to society through their work. Or providing food for their family members. Or immersing themselves in nature. The possibilities are endless. So, the children need to come up with their own ideas about how to make themselves happy. Likewise, when you have an abstract word like "happiness" in your mind, try to make the specific meaning clear to yourself and then think about what action steps are required to make that happen. Other examples of abstract words are "respect" and "harmony." What kind of behaviors do you see when people behave with respect and harmony? Is your definition of them the same as other

よう、英語で行うミーティングの前に、この「アナログからデジタル」の過程を使って、発言や質問を用意されてはいかがでしょうか。

　私たちの頭の中にイメージはあっても、それらのイメージを事実やアイデア、具体的な行動を示す言葉に翻訳するのは容易ではありません。イメージが役立たないと言っているワケではありません。むしろその逆です！ イメージの内容を相手にきちんと伝えることができれば、イメージは非常に有効なものになります。
　また、海外の人が常にデジタル・モードで話すわけではありません。たとえば、アメリカ人の親は子どもによく「幸せであってほしい」と言います。しかし、「幸せ」が何を意味するかは、人によって違います。自由時間を楽しいことに使うことだと言う人もいれば、仕事を通じて社会に貢献することだと言う人もいるでしょう。または、家族にひもじい思いをさせないことだと言う人もいるでしょう。自然にひたることかもしれません。可能性は無限です。ですから、子どもたちが自分を幸せにするにはどうすればいいのか、自分で見当をつけなければなりません。同様に、頭の中に「幸せ」のように抽象的な言葉が浮かんだ場合、それをまず自分の中で明確にし、その上でそれを実現するにはどのようなアクション・ステップを踏めばよいのかを考えてみてください。他の抽象的な言葉の例に、「尊重」「調和」があります。もし人が尊重と調和をもって行動するとしたら、どんな行動になって表れるでしょうか？ あなたの行動定義は他の英語スピーカーのものと同一ですか？ 共通点もあるでしょうが、まったく同じではないか

English speakers'? There may be some commonality, but your and their definitions may not match completely. This is also why we need to digitize our analogue images, so that we can make concrete requests and earn our conversation partners' understanding of the things we say.

Analogue mode is largely based on feelings. In the previous example, when my client selected a number using the scale of one to ten, he/she may have picked a number based on his/her feelings. You may say that the numbers are digital information; however, they still reside in the analogue realm when your conversation partners don't quite understand what you mean.

Analogue perception is valuable, because it comes from all of your past experiences and feelings. It can become even more useful in communication, when you express your analogue perception in concrete words that can give others a better understanding of what you mean.

Generally speaking, people in the Western world are good at digital perception, and expressing it clearly with words. So, Westerners who are used to receiving digital information may get frustrated when Japanese stop talking before giving any specifics about what they mean. For example:

> We need to do better.
>
> We should get this done soon.
>
> We need to complete this.

You need to express what makes it "better," when you think the deadline should be, and what the criteria are for the

もしれません。行動定義に個人差があるのも、要求を具体化し内容を理解してもらうために、アナログ・イメージのデジタル化が必要な理由です。

　アナログ・モードは主に気持ちや感覚に基づいています。クライアントが1から10の間の数字を選んだ例では、クライアントは自分の感覚に基づいて選んだかもしれません。もしかするとあなたは、数字はデジタル情報だとおっしゃるかもしれません。しかし、もしあなたの対話相手があなたの言うことをしっかり理解できないとしたら、その数字はまだアナログの領域にとどまっているのです。

　アナログ知覚は、あなたの過去のすべての経験と感覚から得られる情報ですから、非常に価値があります。あなたのアナログ知覚情報を具体的な言葉で表現できれば、あなたの言いたいことをもっとよくわかってもらえますから、コミュニケーションで非常に役立ちます。

　一般に欧米の人はデジタル知覚と、知覚したものを言葉で明確に表現することに長けています。ですから、デジタル情報を受け取ることに慣れている欧米人は、日本人が意味を具体的に示す前に話を終えてしまうと、イライラします。

　　　　もっと頑張んないとダメだ。

　　　　早めにしあげないといけない。

　　　　これを完了しなければならない。

　何をすれば「ベター」になるのか、締め切りは「いつ」にすればいいのか、作業の「完了」の基準は何なのかを、はっきりと伝える

"completion" of a task.

When I speak with Japanese managers who are working in the U.S., sometimes they say something like, "We need to take good care of people." I'd ask, "what does that mean to you?" "Well, I'll be kind and cognizant of their needs." "How are you going to learn their needs?" We need to explore and define our own images, so that we can make the best use of them when communicating in English (and in Japanese, too).

Explore your own images, digitize, them and convey them in clear terms in at least three sentences. I believe this can also help our communication with our fellow Japanese.

Manners for positive communication

On a Wednesday, I had a video conference call scheduled for 9:00 am. This was my first conference call with a new client. Usually another mother in the neighborhood takes our sons to middle school, but she was not available that morning, so I had to drive them to school. I thought that I could pick up the boys at 7:45, drop them off a bit early, and make it home by 8:00. However, my son reminded me that I needed to drop the boys off between 8:06 and 8:10 am. I felt my shoulder muscles tighten up. The window was very narrow, and did not accommodate working parents. In addition, traffic around the school would be bad. I returned home at 8:15 and glanced in

必要があります。

　アメリカで働く日本人の管理職と話すと、ときどき「従業員の面倒をよく見なければならない」と言うのを聞きます。「あなたにとって、それはどういう意味ですか？」「そうですね、親切で従業員のニーズに気づいてあげることです」「どうやって彼らのニーズを知るのですか？」とまた質問を返します。英語の（日本語でも）コミュニケーションでイメージを最大限に役立てるには、イメージの可能性を追求して、イメージを具体的に定義する必要があります。

　自分の頭の中にあるイメージを追求しデジタル化した上で、英語で3文以上話して伝えます。このやり方は、日本人どうしのコミュニケーションでも有効だと思います。

プラス志向のコミュニケーション作法

　ある水曜日、朝の9時からビデオ会議がありました。これは、新しいクライアントとの初めての会議でした。通常、近所のお母さんが私の息子や男の子たちを学校に送って行きますが、彼女の都合が悪く、その日は私が連れて行くことになりました。7時45分に男の子たちを車に乗せて、少し早めに中学校で降ろし、家に8時には帰ってこられると見積もりました。ところが当日の朝、中学校に着く時間は朝の8時6分から8時10分の間に指定されていると、息子が念を押してきました。肩の筋肉がこわばるのを感じました。時間帯が狭すぎて融通がきかないのは、働く親には不便です。学校周辺の車も多くなり、帰宅に時間がかかります。8時15分に帰宅し、鏡を見ると、ストレスを感じ、疲れ、元気のない

the mirror. I looked stressed, tired, and not very happy. So, I took a quick hot shower to refresh my mind, put on makeup, using more than I usually do, and practiced smiling to myself in the mirror. The conference call went well, but it turned out that we couldn't use the video. An incident like this is called "Murphy's Law," which means that anything that can go wrong will go wrong. But my point here is that you may also want to put your best foot forward when you want to give others a good impression of yourself.

This is especially important when you meet someone for the first time. You can only make a first impression once. Also, non-Japanese who don't expect to have long relationships at work due to employee mobility (such as finding a new role within the same company, finding a new job at a different company, changing a career or place to live, or retiring) tend to judge you via first impressions.

Path to Mastery 8

1. Eye contact

Try to keep eye contact for at least five seconds (please also see p.166).

2. Other facial expressions

When your eyes meet another person's eyes, smile a bit. This shows both your friendliness and your confidence.

3. Posture

顔が映っていました。それで熱いシャワーをさっと浴びて気分転換をし、いつもより厚めに化粧をし、鏡に向かってにっこり笑う練習をしました。会議はうまくいきましたが、ビデオをONにできず、厚化粧の甲斐はありませんでした。余談ですが、このような出来事を「マーフィーの法則」と呼びます。悪い方向へいく可能性があるものはすべて現実になる、という意味です。それはともあれ、ここで私が申し上げたいのは、よい印象を与えたいときは、自分のベストを尽くすべきだ、ということです。

これは、人と初めて会うときは特に大切なことです。第一印象を与えるチャンスは一回しかありません。また、海外では、同じ会社の別の職務に移ったり、転職したり、仕事の内容を全く変えて別のキャリアを目指したり、引っ越したり、引退したりと従業員の移動が多く、職場で長期的な人間関係を期待できないため、彼らは第一印象で人を判断しがちです。

コミュニケーションの極意 8 ［第一印象を大切に］

1. アイ・コンタクト（相手の目を見る）

最低5秒は視線を合わせたままにします（p.167参照）。

2. その他の表情

人と目が合ったとき、ほんのすこし微笑むようにします。そうすることで、相手に対する親しみと自分の自信を表現できます。

3. 姿勢

Please don't fold your arms and look down as you listen to others. This is a closed posture in the Western world, and suggests that you're not open to different opinions.

4. Voice

Raise your voice by 20 percent. Avoid mumbling words. Please speak clearly at your own pace.

5. Appearance

I had a session with a Japanese couple who had both come to the U.S. for work. The husband had a beard that looked as if it had been untouched for a long time. The wife thought it was not good for business, and asked me to advise him on it. This was rather personal, and I would have rather avoided the question all together; however, the wife was really concerned about this, so I provided a few points. In general, facial hair that looks "unplanned" doesn't give others a positive impression of you. Uncombed hair, long nose hair, or a beard where the shape is not well defined can give the impression that you don't take care of yourself, and therefore, you can't take care of others or your business. You don't have to look fabulous, unless you want to. But we can all try to look nice and pleasant by taking care of our looks before we go out the door.

6. How to shake hands

When you shake hands, hold your counterpart's hand with one hand, and hold it strongly. You can shake hands up and down twice, and then release your counterpart's hand. If you stepped forward to shake hands, you need to step back when you release your hand, in order to keep the comfortable proximity, about the arm's length. Avoid

人の話を聞くとき、腕を組んで下を見るのはやめましょう。これは欧米では「閉じた姿勢」で、違う意見に耳を貸さない態度の表れと考えられています。

4. 声

日本語で話しているときと比べて、音量を20パーセント上げてください。もごもごと話すのはいただけません。自分のペースではっきりと話しましょう。

5. 外観

ある日のクライアントは、二人ともアメリカに赴任してきた日本人のご夫婦でした。ご主人は口ひげがありましたが、まるで長い間ひげを剃っていないように見えました。奥さんは彼の見た目がビジネスには適切ではないと考えていて、私にアドバイスをしてくれるよう頼んできました。これは個人的な問題なので、口を挟みたくなかったのですが、彼女は本当に心配しているようでした。それで、ポイントを2、3伝えました。一般に、「自然のまま」の状態に見える顔の毛は、ポジティブな印象を与えません。櫛を通していない髪や、長い鼻毛や形の整っていないひげは、その人が自分の頭の上のハエも追えない人で、人やビジネスの管理はできないだろうという印象を与えます。もちろん、素晴らしい見栄えを目指してもかまいませんが、そこまでしなくとも大丈夫です。けれども家の玄関を出る前に、清潔感と感じのよさを醸し出す努力をしましょう。

6. 握手

握手をするときは、相手の手を片手で強く握ってください。上下に2回軽く振って（振らなくても可）、手をすぐ放すようにします。相手に一歩近づいて握手した場合は、握手が終わったら元の場所に戻り、相手と腕の長さほどの適切な距離を保つようにします。相手の手を両方の手で長く握らないようにしま

holding your counterpart's hand with both hands for a long time. Most Westerners feel strange with such an intimate handshake. Also, a handshake that is too soft can give your counterpart the image of a "dead fish" and they may think that you are not confident. Overall, a strong and short handshake can communicate your honesty and confidence.

7. How to eat

Please avoid speaking while you have food in your mouth. I'm guilty of this sometimes, because I'm a very slow eater and keep food in my mouth for a long time. I should be careful about this.

Please remember BMW (bread, main dish, and wine or water). If there is a little plate on your right side, it isn't yours. Your little plate for bread is always on your left side. Likewise, your water and other drinks are on your right side. Keep your knife and fork separate while you're still eating. Put the knife and fork together on your plate when you're done with the dish.

8. When you have a cold

Even when you have a cold, please say "good," "not bad," or "okay," if you're at work and someone asks you, "How are you?" Most Westerners don't like to be miserable at work or to deal with someone who is miserable. Once you're there, you need to show your strength and confidence that you can do your work well.

9. Special notes for Japanese gentlemen

Please don't pull up your pants in front of others. This is something little boys can do and can even look cute, but if adult men do it, that can make others uncomfortable.

しょう。ほとんどの欧米人は、そのような握手に過度の親近感を感じ、居心地が悪くなります。また、握り方がゆるすぎると、相手の人は「死んだ魚」を握ったかのように感じ、また、あなたのことを自信のない人と考えてしまうかもしれません。要するに、強くて短い握手で、あなたの正直な人柄と自信を伝えることができます。

7. 食べ方

口に食べ物を入れたまま話さないようにしてください。食べるのが遅い私は、長い間食べ物を口に含んでいるので、ときどきこれをやってしまいます。私も気をつけます。

BMW（bread パン、main dish 主菜を載せる大皿、そして wine/water ワインかお水）と覚えてください。もしあなたの右側に小さなお皿がある場合、それはあなたのパン皿ではありません。あなたのパン皿は、いつも左側にあります。同様に、あなたの水と他の飲み物は右側にあります。まだ食べている間は、フォークとナイフはカタカナの「ハ」の形のように分けて置きます。料理を食べ終わったら、フォークとナイフを揃えてお皿の上に置きます。

8. 風邪を引いているとき

風邪を引いているときでも、職場で誰かに「気分はどう？」と聞かれたら、「よい」「悪くない」「オーケー」と答えましょう。ほとんどの欧米人は、みじめなのが嫌いで、また、みじめな人を煙たがります。いったん職場に着いたら、業務をきちんとこなす力と自信があることを示すべきです。

9. 日本人紳士への特別メッセージ

人前でズボンを引き上げるのはいただけません。小さな男の子がすると可愛くもありますが、大人の男性がすると、周りの人の居心地が悪くなります。

How to have more air time

I'm talking about how long you are speaking in any occasion, not the number of words that you speak. If you speak 30 minutes in an hour meeting, you had 50 percent of the air time. It is rare for a Japanese to have 50 percent or more air time, as we're from a listening culture, and most English speakers are from speaking cultures. However, in order to ensure that you have a decent exchange of information with your conversation partners, you need to maintain 40 percent of air time. How do you do this?

❖ Path to Mastery 9

1. Speak slowly

If you speak fast, they'll also speak fast, because they will assume that you are a better speaker of English than you may be. If you slow down a bit and speak at your own pace, they may also slow down, and you'll have more opportunities to convey what you mean and ask questions.

2. Ask others to speak slowly

"Excuse me. You are speaking a little too fast for me."

"I'm sorry. Could you please speak more slowly?"

3. Ask what you missed or you didn't understand

"Excuse me. I didn't catch the last sentence. Can you

もっと長く話す

　単語数のことを言っているワケではなく、どれぐらい長い時間話すかということです。もし、1時間のミーティングで30分話したとしたら、あなたは会議時間の50パーセントを占めていたことになります。日本は「聞く文化」で、ネイティブ・スピーカーのほとんどは「話す文化」出身ですから、日本人が50パーセント以上の時間を使えるのはまれです。しかし、情報の交換が十分に行えるよう、40パーセントは時間を確保すべきです。どうすれば、できるのでしょう？

◆ **コミュニケーションの極意 9**　[情報交換を十分に行うには]

1. ゆっくり話す

　早く話すと、実力より高い英語力があると思われて、相手も早く話してきます。ゆっくり自分のペースで話すと、相手もゆっくりめに話してくれ、その結果、言いたいことを伝え、質問をするチャンスが増えます。

2. ゆっくり話してくれるよう頼む

「すみません、あなたの話し方は早すぎます」

「すみません、もう少しゆっくり話していただけますか？」

3. 聞き逃したことやわからなかったことについて尋ねる

「すみません、最後の文が聞き取れませんでした。もう一度

say that again, please?"

"Excuse me. Can you repeat the last thing you said?"

"Excuse me, but what does "harried" mean?"

"Excuse me. I believe you said something like "ca ... caden"?"

When you ask questions, timing is the most important thing. If you don't say "excuse me" right away, the "last sentence" will be several sentences ago.

4. Ask for more explanation

"I'm sorry I don't follow you. Can you explain how part A is connected with part B?"

"Why do we need to do this first instead of checking the product availability?"

"What do you mean by "all"?"

When you hear or say words like "all" and "everything," it is better to define those words right there, in order to make sure that both sides are talking about the same thing.

"Will"

Before coming to the U.S., I had learned that the word "will" expresses the speaker's willingness. So, whenever I was asked to do something for another department, I would respond, "Yes, I will." Then one day a consultant on the same

言ってもらえますか？」

「すみません、最後の文をもう一度くり返してもらえますか？」

「すみません、『harried』の意味は何ですか？」

「すみません、先ほど『ca ……caden』のような単語を聞いたのですが?」

　質問をする上で一番大事なのはタイミングです。「すみません！」と即座に言わないと、「最後の文」はしばらく前に聞いた文になってしまいます。

4. 詳しい説明を求める

「すみません、話の筋を追えませんでした。パートAとパートBはどう関連しているのですか？」

「製品の準備状況を確認する前に、どうしてこれをする必要があるのですか？」

「『すべて』とは何を意味するのでしょう？」

　「all」や「everything」と言ったり聞いたりした場合は、その場ですぐに内容の定義をして、双方の理解に誤差が生じないようにしてください。

「Will」を使うときの注意

　アメリカに来る前、「will」は話し手のやる気を表現すると学びました。それで、他の部署の人に何かを頼まれると、「Yes, I will.」と答えていました。するとある日、同じ階のコンサルタントが聞いてきたのです。「どうやら、これをしたくなさそうだね」これに

floor asked me "So, it doesn't seem like you want to do this." I was shocked, and it must've shown on my face. He quickly provided his explanation: I said "will" so often that I sounded as though I was not willing or that I was upset with having to do the task.

I'm sure that my tone of voice wasn't right either; my happily pronounced "will" must have sounded like I was saying, "I know I should do this, don't say it again!" So, I changed my response to the following:

"Sure. I'm happy to do it."

"I'm going to do it this afternoon."

"Of course. When do you need to have the results?"

"I'm a little tied up now. Can this wait until tomorrow morning?"

Japanese "Yes"

This question always comes up when I train groups of Americans or coach individual Americans on how to communicate with Japanese: Do Japanese mean "no" when they say "yes"? This is largely because we tend to say "yes" when we say *hai* in Japanese. Japanese *hai* means "I'm listening, so keep talking." But most non-Japanese take the Japanese "yes" as a sign of understanding or agreement. And they are surprised when they get similar questions from

はびっくりしました。きっと顔にそれが出たのでしょう、彼はすぐ説明してくれました。私が「will」を頻繁に使ったので、やる気がないか、作業を頼まれたことでムッとしているように響いたというのです。

　私の語調も悪かったのだと思います。明るく発音したつもりの「will」は、「これをしなきゃいけないことはわかってます。二度と言わないでください！」のように聞こえたに違いありません。それで、対応を以下のように変えました。

　「もちろん。よろこんでしますよ」

　「今日の午後に取り掛かります」

　「もちろん。いつまでにしあげればよいですか？」

　「ちょっと今忙しいので、明日の朝までにしあげるということでよいですか？」

日本人の「イエス」

　アメリカ人のグループをトレーニングするとき、または個人をコーチングするとき、必ずこの質問を受けます。日本人が「イエス」というとき、本当は「ノー」を意味するんですか？　これは主に、日本語で「はい」と言う場面で、英語で「イエス」と言ってしまうからです。日本語の「はい」は、「聞いてますから、話を続けてください」という意味です。しかし海外の人はこの日本人の「イエス」を、理解もしくは合意の印と受け取ります。そして、日本人から３日前と似た質問をくり返されると、びっくりしてしまい

Japanese that they talked to three days ago. Please say "yes" less frequently to avoid misunderstanding. Also, try to replace "yes (*hai*)" with "uh-huh" that you pronounce with a rising tone.

Say "uh-huh" instead of "yes" if you're just listening.

Never say "no" too quickly when you get a chance to say something

In a questionnaire, how do you usually answer the question, "What information would you like to have?" I often see "no" written by Japanese. Maybe they didn't think it was an important question, or they didn't have time to think about it. But they missed a great chance to talk about themselves. Whenever you see a question, please give yourself some time to think about it. Americans see this type of question as a chance to address their own specific needs and will try to make the most of it.

Suppose someone asked you the same question in a meeting, and you didn't think of anything to ask. Then, you may want to say something like the following:

"Well, I can't think of any at the moment. However, I'm concerned about … "

"I'm sure I'll have questions once I start doing the work."

"Thank you. I first need to absorb what I've learned today.

ます。誤解を避けるために、「イエス」という回数を減らしてください。また、「イエス（はい）」を音を上げつつ言う「アハ（ハの音のほうがアより高い）」に変えてください。

　聞いているだけなら、「イエス」ではなく「アハ」で相づちを打ちます。

話すチャンスのとき、あっさり「ノー」と言わない

　「どんな情報がほしいですか？」というアンケートの質問に、普段どう答えていますか？　日本人が「特になし」と書いているのをよく見ます。重要な質問と思わなかったのかもしれませんし、考える時間がなかったのかもしれません。いずれにしても、自分のことについて話す（書く）よいチャンスを逃したのです。質問を見たら、必ず時間をかけて考えてください。アメリカ人はこのような質問を、自分の特定のニーズについて書くよいチャンスだと考え、最大限に利用しようとします。

　仮に、同じ質問をミーティングで受けたとします。でも、特に必要な情報を思いつきませんでした。そのような場合、以下のように対応するのがいいでしょう。

　「特に何も思いつきませんが、気になっていることがあります」

　「作業を始めたら、きっと質問が出てくると思います」
　「ありがとうございます。まず、今日学んだことを吸収したい

Can I get back to you later with any questions?"

If you can't come up with a relevant question, then the next best thing is to keep the channel open for further communication.

Positive look on life in general

In order to explain one of the differences between Japanese and American views, I draw a glass that is filled up to exactly 50 percent of its height. Americans tend to see this as "half-full," and Japanese tend to see the same as "half-empty." Japanese and Americans who are looking at the same spreadsheet showing the progress of a project can have two different sentiments: we have already done the first half or we still have to go another half. This slight difference can create differences in views and attitudes toward the same project or task. I said before that a positive attitude alone usually can't solve an issue. However, it doesn't hurt to have a positive attitude.

と思います。後で質問してもいいですか？」

　もし、関連の質問を思いつかなければ、その後のコミュニケーションの流れを確保するよう努めてください。

人生全般に対する前向きな見方

　日本とアメリカの見方の違いの一つを説明するために、水がコップの高さのきっちり半分まで入っている絵を描きます。アメリカ人はこれを、「半分も入っている」と見がちで、日本人は「半分しか入っていない」と見ます。プロジェクトの進捗を示す同じ表を見ている日本人とアメリカ人が、「もう半分終わった」か「あと半分も残っている」と、違う感覚を持つことがあります。このちょっとした違いが、同じプロジェクトや作業に対し異なる見方や態度を生むことがあります。通常、態度が前向きなだけでは案件を解決できないと申し上げましたが、プラス志向の態度で、損することもありません。

❖ Summary ❖

Two-way communication doesn't happen if you are mostly listening. (If it's a one-way communication, it would become a "lecture.") If you think that you haven't talked enough before, then, you need to speak more. Preparation and practice will help you get used to two-way communication.

Always aim for communication through which others will be interested in you and that helps you further develops good relationships.

Once you start talking (writing), keep speaking (writing) for at least three sentences.

Let's try the following:

- In preparation for a meeting, digitize the message and information that you want to convey.

- Practice: First clearly state what you've understood and then ask questions.

- Practice: Adapt to non-verbal behaviors shared by English speakers. Speaking in English in front of a mirror with body language and hand gesture may be helpful.

聞き役ばかりに回っていると、双方向のコミュニケーションにならない（一方通行の場合は「講義」）。今まで話し足りなかったと感じているのなら、もっと話すことが大切。慣れるまでは、準備と練習が必要。

相手に興味をもってもらえるコミュニケーション、よい人間関係につながるコミュニケーションを心がけよう。

話しだしたら（書きだしたら）、最低でも３文は話す（書く）。

やってみよう

・人に会う前に、伝えたいメッセージや情報のデジタル化をして準備。

・理解した点を明確に伝えてから質問をする練習を。

・アイコンタクトや姿勢など、非言語スタイルも英語文化に適応させる練習を。鏡の前で、身振り手振りを加えて英語で話すのもいい練習。

Chapter III

Small Talk

As soon as I moved to the U.S., I found myself having very brief and very frequent conversations with strangers. We discussed the same things over and over, as they asked me the same questions, such as "How are you?" "What do you do for living?" "What are you trained for?" "What do you think of America?" "Where did you grow up?" and so on. I wondered if Americans were only interested in those subjects. I also wondered if they were disappointed in my answers, because they didn't seem to be interested in having a longer and more meaningful conversation. Not that it would have been possible though, as I was barely able to respond with a "yes" or "no" to their questions at that time.

Most Asians find these short conversations somewhat awkward and challenging, because we tend to take a longer time to get to know each other by asking gentle questions and

第3章

スモールトーク（世間話）

　アメリカに引っ越すとすぐ、初対面の人と、とても短い会話を頻繁にすることになりました。毎回違う相手から、「元気？」「お仕事は何？」「どんな教育を受けたの？」「アメリカのことをどう思う？」「どこで育ったの？」などの同じ質問をされたので、私は同じことについて何度も話すことになりました。アメリカ人は他の事に興味はないのだろうか、と訝りました。また、もっと長く話してお互いを知り合うことに興味がなさそうだったので、私の返事にがっかりしたのだろうかとも思いました。もっとも、その頃は相手の質問に「イエス」か「ノー」で答えるのがやっとだったので、長くて意味のある会話が可能だったワケではないのですが。

　アジア人のほとんどは、思いやりのある質問を通じて、または一緒に過ごす中で、時間をかけてお互いを知り合うので、短い対話をやりずらいと感じたり、難しいと思ったりします。しかし欧

spending more time together. However, most people in the Western world get to know each other through a type of short, rather abrupt conversation called "small talk." This "small talk" holds the key to developing a wider range of relationships as well as deepening existing relationships with others. And this small talk can give you a big challenge.

There are several reasons why small talk gives us such a headache, and I would like to recommend several things to mitigate that headache.

Understand what small talk is

We have a certain image of the word "conversation" in our native language. In Japan, it usually takes place in a relaxed atmosphere when we are not rushed. You're sitting at a table and talking over coffee or lunch or after-work drinks or even dinner. But small talk is different. You're usually standing as you are engaged in it, and you may be on your way to somewhere else.

Think of small talk as a concise PR of yourself. You're figuratively selling yourself through information about yourself that you want to share. In other words, you can be selective regarding what you talk about. Some Japanese are hesitant to share information about their private life, especially in an open place like a hallway. But remember one of the key

米人の多くは、「スモールトーク（世間話）」と呼ばれる、話題が
コロコロ変わる短い会話を通じてお互いを知り合います。このス
モールトークこそが、人間関係を深めるだけでなく、広い範囲の
人と知り合うための鍵を握っているのです。そして、この短い話
が、あなたの大きな悩みの種になる可能性が大きいのです。

　頭痛の原因がいくつかあります。本章では、それに対処し頭痛
を和らげる方法を紹介します。

スモールトークとは？

　私たちは、自分の母国語の「対話」という言葉に対して、あるイ
メージを抱いています。日本ではたいてい、急かされない、ゆっ
たりした雰囲気の中で行うものというイメージがあります。テー
ブルに座って、コーヒーを飲みながら、またはランチを食べなが
ら、仕事の後に一杯やりながら、夕食をともにしながら話すとい
う感じです。けれども、スモールトークは違います。たいていは
立ったままするもので、参加者はそれぞれ、どこかへ向かう途中
かもしれません。

　スモールトークを、短い自己PRと考えてください。比喩的な
意味ですが、自分に関する情報を知ってもらうことで、自分とい
う商品を売るのです。言い換えれば、何について話すかは、あな
たの選択しだいなのです。日本人の中には、自分の個人的な生活
について、他人と、しかも廊下のような公的な場所で話すのをた
めらう人もいます。けれども、重要なことは「話す内容は自分で

words here is "selective." Other key words are "short" and for "public consumption." In most cases, people in the Western world are not interested in truly private subjects. So, please find something positive and fun that you do and that you don't mind sharing. Topics that work well include:

Path to Mastery 10

- Weather

- Sports

- Hobbies

- Movies that you enjoyed

- TV shows that you follow

- Your children or pet (yes, these are private topics, however, these are also common human interests. You don't have to talk about this, if you don't want to.)

- Fun activities that you've done recently (a barbeque, a concert, a hike and so on)

- Non-political news that has caught your attention

In the last several weeks, my friends and I talked about the following topics:

- Minor health issues, like allergies

- Minor financial pain caused by children who order very expensive dishes at restaurants

選択する」ということです。そして、「短い」「公にしていい情報」であることも大切です。ほとんどの場合、欧米の人は、本当に個人的な類の話には興味がありません。ですから、あなたが経験することの中で、人に話してもかまわない、前向きで楽しい事について話してください。

◆ **コミュニケーションの極意 10** ［おすすめのスモールトーク］

- 天気

- スポーツ

- 趣味

- 面白かった映画

- 継続して見ているテレビ番組

- 子どもやペット（これは個人的な話題ですが、多くの人が興味のある話題です。話したくなければ、話題にする必要はありません）

- 最近経験した面白い出来事（バーベキュー、コンサート、ハイキングなど）

- 政治以外の耳寄りなニュース

　以下は、この数週間の中で、友だちとの世間話に出てきた話題です。

- アレルギーなどの、ちょっとした健康問題

- レストランで子どもが高額の料理を頼み、高くついて参ったこと

- An effort to catch stray cats and have them neutered by a veterinarian

- Plans for the summer

- Supplements that help our kids grow

- Celebrities' plastic surgery and how far we would want to go if we had the money

- A news story regarding an illegal immigrant in France who scaled an apartment building and saved a toddler dangling off a balcony

- A jewelry party that one of my friends is planning to host

- A Korean spa that one of my friends enthusiastically recommends

So, it's nothing overly exciting, but it can be funny and it is something that most people can relate to. Alternatively, you can also talk about your unique experiences or interests. I remember a Japanese who talked about his experience teaching children in his neighborhood how to beat Japanese drums for local festivals. Or you can talk about your unique take on a hobby or activity, like fishing. One of the Japanese businessmen said that he enjoys the thrill of seeing what kind of fish will appear when he pulls it out of the ocean. Fishing brings him joy in two ways: he enjoys the mystery of not knowing what kind of fish will appear, and then eating it! Both conversations left a positive and lasting impression on me.

- 野良猫を捕まえて動物病院で避妊手術をさせる苦労

- 夏休みの計画

- 子どもの成長を助けるサプリメント

- 芸能人の美容整形手術と、もしお金があったらどこまで整形するか

- フランスで不法移民がアパートの壁をよじ登り、バルコニーから吊り下がっていた幼児を救助したニュース

- 友だちの一人が企画している宝石パーティー（食べたり飲んだりしながら宝石を見る、社交的ショッピング・パーティー）

- 友だちの一人が熱心に薦めるコリアン・スパ

　特にワクワクするというわけではありませんが、笑える話題や、その場にいるほとんどの人が興味のありそうな話題です。また逆に、珍しい経験や興味のある事柄について話すのもいいでしょう。近所のお祭りのために、子どもたちに和太鼓の叩き方を教えた経験について話した日本人のことを、今も覚えています。または、魚釣りなど、自分の趣味や活動に対する独自の見方について話すのもいいでしょう。釣り糸を海から引き揚げながら、どんな魚が現れるのかとワクワクする瞬間が楽しいと言った、日本人ビジネスマンもいました。彼は魚釣りに二つの喜びを感じるそうです。どんな魚が現れるかわからないミステリー。そしてそれを食べる喜び！ この二人とのスモールトークは、思い出すたびに楽しくなります。

Basic manners of small talk

■ Basic Manners　[1]
Keep it upbeat

Remember small talk is your PR, so think about some subjects that can project a positive image of you. Sometimes, though, you may find yourself inadvertently talking about a less than ideal situation or experience. For example, someone asked about your lost key or injury or sick cat. When that happens, try to find a silver lining to your experience.

"I'm glad it's behind me."

"Well, my nose will be straighter than before! (after you broke your nose)"

"Thanks for asking. My cat is doing better."

"I'm good now. Thanks! It's good to be back!"

Keep in mind that small talk is for public consumption, so you may want to keep serious topics for another occasion.

■ Basic Manners　[2]
Keep it short

To give good PR of yourself in small talk, you need to pay

スモールトークの基本作法

明るく元気に

　スモールトークはPRですから、自分のポジティブなイメージ
を投影できる話題を考えましょう。とはいっても、時には思わず、
困った状況や格好の悪い経験を話すハメになってしまうことも
あります。たとえば、失くした鍵や、ケガ、病気の猫などについ
て聞かれたときなどです。そんなことになってしまったら、困っ
た経験の中に何か明るいニュースを探してみてください。

> 「とにかく終わって、よかった」

> 「前より鼻が真っすぐになるだろう！（鼻の骨を折ってしまっ
> 　た後）」

> 「聞いてくれてありがとう。うちの猫は前より調子がいいよ」

> 「もうすっかり元気だよ。ありがとう。戻ってこれて、うれしい！」

　スモールトークは不特定多数の人と共有してもかまわない内
容のものですから、慎重さを要する内容の話題は、別の機会に
したほうがいいでしょう。

短く

　スモールトークがよいPRになるよう、その目的（情報を公にす

attention to the purpose (public consumption), what to talk about (be selective), and its length (be brief). The first two are relatively easy, as you can handle them intellectually. The third one, "be brief," is the most important and challenging for most Asians. You want others to understand the circumstances of your story, and why this particular topic is important to you. And this common mode (high context) makes your small talk a little too long. Most Westerners, especially Americans, have little patience for this, as they expect small talk to be short. So, for example, you don't want to talk about why you decided to go fishing. Instead, talk about the fish you caught or the fish you bought on your way home! If they're interested, they'll ask you questions. By responding to those questions, you may be able to tell them the whole story.

You may worry that you'll sound abrupt or even rude, if you speak in this short format. That is a legitimate concern. With positive non-verbal expressions though, you'll be able to reduce the risk of others misinterpreting or taking offense. The non-verbal expressions include the tone of your voice and your facial expressions. Even if you're afraid that your English may have been a bit choppy, your facial expression can communicate that you appreciated their company, and you can be assured that you gave yourself some good PR.

る）と話題（取捨選択をする）、長さ（短くまとめる）に注意してください。最初の二つは理解すれば対処できるので、比較的簡単です。三つ目の短くまとめるというのが一番重要で、かつアジア人の多くが苦労する点です。あなたの置かれた状況、そしてなぜ特定の話題があなたにとって重要かを相手に理解してもらいたいと思うからです。そして、このアジア人にありがちなモード（ハイ・コンテクスト*）がスモールトークを長くしてしまうのです。欧米人、特にアメリカ人は短い話を期待していますから、長い話を最後まで我慢して聞けません。ですから、たとえば魚釣りに行くことにした理由については省くほうが賢明です。そのかわりに、釣った魚か、家に帰る途中で買った魚について話してください。もし彼らが興味をそそられれば、質問してきます。その質問に答えることで、まとまった話を伝えることができるでしょう。

　短く話すことで、ぶっきらぼうに、あるいは失礼に響くのではないかと心配されるかもしれません。そのご心配はもっともです。しかし、ポジティブな非言語コミュニケーションで、誤解やムッとされるリスクを軽減できます。非言語表現には、声音や顔の表情などがあります。滑らかな英語が話せなくても、相手と一緒に話すのを楽しんでいることを声や表情で伝えることができれば、よいPRになったと思って間違いありません。

＊話の内容に、状況や今までの経緯などの情報が多く盛り込まれたコミュニケーションのこと。欧米人は一般にロー（low）・コンテクストで、結論とそれを支える理由を中心に述べ、状況や経緯の説明にはあまり時間を割かない。

Topics to avoid

Culture is like air. You are not aware of your own culture until you're devoid of it by moving to a different country/region or detect something different or uncomfortable in your own culture (generational gaps, for example).

In hierarchical societies, which are common throughout Asia, we tend to pay more attention to a person's rank or age. However, as you may know, if you ask about someone's age, you can be seen as encroaching upon his or her privacy. And that is not good PR. In order to make small talk work for you, I strongly recommend that you avoid the following topics, at least initially.

- Age
- Marital status
- Sexual orientation
- Political and religious affiliations

How to participate in small talk

There are some cultural obstacles that we need to go over. This is because we assume that certain formats of "conversation" are normal, and we need to develop a new attitude towards "small talk."

避けるべき話題

　文化は空気のようなものです。違う国や地域に引越すか、または自国の文化の中で何かが違うと察したり、違和感を感じたり（たとえば世代の差など）するまで、自分の文化を意識しないものです。

　アジアに多い縦社会では、人の地位や年齢に注目しがちです。しかし、ご存じかもしれませんが、欧米諸国では誰かに年齢を聞くと、その人のプライバシー侵害になりかねません。そうなると、よいPRではなくなってしまいます。PR効果のあるスモールトークのために、少なくとも出会ってしばらくの間は、以下の話題を避けてください。

- 年齢
- 結婚しているかどうか
- 性的指向（異性愛者か同性愛者かなど）
- 属したり支援している政治団体や宗教団体など

スモールトークに参加するには

　乗り越えなければならない文化的な障害がいくつかあります。これは、わたしたち日本人が一定の形式の「対話」を当たり前と考えるからです。ですから、「スモールトーク」に対する新しい姿勢を身につける必要があります。

You can disrupt the flow

In Japanese conversation, we try to go with the flow of conversations that are already in progress. If you apply this attitude to small talk, you'll probably have very few chances to speak about yourself. Yes, you need to let others have time for their PR, but you also need to create opportunities for your own PR. Otherwise, they may see you as unfriendly or antisocial, and you may end up missing the chance to develop a good relationship. Small talk can be a bit abrupt. If you start talking about something totally different, they may be surprised, but they may also find it refreshing, and most of all they will appreciate the fact that you're willing to share things about yourself.

You can oppose someone's view

Small talk can be used to show who you are by telling others where you don't agree. This can be done without being offensive or defensive. You can say, for example, "Well, my experience is different," and then tell them about your experience. Or give reasons for why you disagree, such as, "I know that tapas are 'in' now, but I like regular restaurants where I can enjoy one or two favorite dishes, rather than

会話の流れを乱してもよい

　日本語の会話では、すでに始まっている会話の流れに沿うようにします。もしこの姿勢をアメリカ流のスモールトークに適用すると、自分のことを話すチャンスはほとんど巡ってきません。もちろん、他の人にもPRさせてあげるべきですが、自分のPRのための機会も作る必要があります。そうでないと、親近感の足りない人、対人恐怖症の人などと思われてしまい、よい人間関係を築く機会を逃してしまいます。スモールトークは多少ぶっきらぼうでもかまいません。もし、あなたが現在の話題とまったく違うことを話し始めたら、周りの人はびっくりするかもしれません。けれども、新鮮だと感じるかもしれませんし、何よりも、自分のことについて話そうとするあなたの意欲をアメリカ人は好意的に評価します。

人の意見に反対してもよい

　スモールトークを通じて、賛成できない内容を示し、自分の人となりを伝えることもできます。これは相手を攻撃したり、自分を防衛したりせずにできることです。たとえば、「私の経験は違います」と話します。そのあとに続けて、自分の経験談を披露します。または、「タパスが人気なのは知ってるけど、小皿料理をいくつも頼み続けるより、レストランで自分の好きな料理を一つか二つ食べるほうがいいな」のように、反対理由を話します。当たり

constantly ordering small dishes." Obviously, you don't want to go against everyone's views all the time, however, exchanging different views and experiences is healthy. Others will learn, for example, that Steve likes seafood, but Takeshi doesn't like sushi; he is not a typical Japanese! This is a great opportunity to let them know what you like or dislike, how you see things, and your preferred approach towards things, both in work and life in general.

■ Tips for Making Small Talk [3]

Keep a good rhythm

The rhythm of small talk is like playing catch. You get a ball and toss it in the air a few times, and then you throw it to another person. In other words, you need to know when to let go. You talked about something they don't know—Japanese tea ceremony for example. If nobody asked you a question, then you should recognize that this particular group of people is not into tea ceremony, and let it go. Please try to see this in a positive light: they learned something about you, and you learned that they're not into Japanese tea ceremony. You can leverage this knowledge in your next small talk.

You can't talk fast in English? Neither can I. You don't have to worry too much about it. However, please try to reduce the "thinking time." Thinking about topics ahead of time is good preparation. If you practice this for a few weeks, it'll become

前ですが、人の意見にいつも反対するのはおすすめできません。しかし、違った考えや経験を交換するのは健全なことです。そうすることで、たとえば、スティーブは海鮮ものが好きだけど、タケシは寿司が嫌いで一風変わった日本人だ、などということがわかってくるのです。あなたが何が好きで嫌いか、あなたのものの見方、仕事や生活全般の物事に対する好みの取り組み方を人にわかってもらうのに、もってこいの機会です。

■参加の姿勢[3]
リズム感よく

スモールトークのリズムは、キャッチボールのリズムと似ています。ボールを受けて、手のひらで二、三回少し上に投げてはつかみ、そのあと別の人に投げます。つまり、ボールを渡すタイミングを知る必要があるのです。たとえば、日本の茶道など、海外の人が知らないことを話したとしましょう。もし誰も質問してこなかったら、その場にいた人たちは茶道には興味がないと理解し、その話題で話し続けるのを諦めるのが得策です。これをどうか、よい方向に解釈してください。その場にいた人たちは、あなたについて何かを知りましたし、あなたも彼らが日本の茶道には興味がないことがわかりました。この知識を次のスモールトークに生かすことができます。

　英語では早く話せないって？　私もです。話すスピードについて、過度の心配は不要です。けれども、「考えている時間」は短縮するようにしてください。話す話題について事前に考えておくの

automatic. You'll notice things that have caught your attention in the news, things you saw on your way to work or during a walk over the weekend, and so on.

And please try to say a word or phrase like "Well," "Oh, right," or "Let me see," almost immediately after you've heard a question. This way others understand that you've received the ball. Having long silences makes others uncomfortable, as you broke the rhythm of "playing catch." Keeping the ball going back and forth at a comfortable rhythm is more important than the speed of your English.

■ Tips for Making Small Talk [4]
Ask questions if you have nothing to offer

Small talk takes some getting used to. Sometimes Japanese find it difficult to come up with new topics. Let's say you come across a group of people in the elevator, and you can't think of anything to talk about. Then, the easiest thing is to let others have the floor. You can nod and ask questions, such as:

"Then, what happened?"

"What are you going to do?"

"The final score was 7–2? The pitcher wasn't good?"

"I've never heard about that. Can you explain more about it?"

"Wow! How did that happen?"

"I've never been there. What did you think?"

は、よい準備になります。数週間ほど実践すると、自然にできるようになります。ニュースではっと思ったことや、出勤途中や週末の散歩のときなどに目にしたことを気に留めるようになります。

　それから、質問を聞いたらすぐに、「Well（えーっと）」とか「Oh right（そうですねぇ）」「Let me see（さてと）」などと言うように心がけてください。そうすることで、他の人はあなたがボールを受け取ったとわかります。長い沈黙があると、キャッチボールのリズムが崩れ、居心地が悪くなってしまいます。英語を話すスピードより、ボールをリズム感よく投げたり受け取ったりすることのほうが大事です。

■参加の姿勢 [４]

何も話すことがなければ、質問をする

　スモールトークには慣れが必要です。新しい話題を提供するのが難しいと思うときもあります。エレベーターで数人と一緒になったとしましょう。話したいことを何も思いつきません。その場合、一番楽なのは、他の人に話してもらうことです。頷いて、質問をします。

　「で、どうなったの？」
　「どうするつもり？」
　「最終得点は７対２？ ピッチャーが悪かったの？」
　「聞いたことないなぁ。もっと説明してくれる？」
　「えぇ! どうしてそんなことになっちゃったの？」
　「行ったことないです。どう思った？」

Or you can make a comment like the following:

"You must be so proud!"
"I wish I had been there."

Most Westerners love these questions/comments because they show your interest in them and their experiences. And of course, it was good PR for you too, as you contributed to the small talk.

How to prepare for small talk

You need to do a lot of self-discovery. Japanese, including myself, are not always aware of what we believe in, our principles for life, and how to approach things. We think that we have to adjust to continuously changing environments and situations as necessary. We also tend to believe that fulfilling our roles at work and home is more important than who we are as individuals. However, most people in the Western world believe that their principles are coherent and steady, and independent of the situation they happen to be in. As a result, if you say, "I'm not sure," or "It all depends," too many times, then they may think that you don't have a back bone. This is not good PR.

Westerners typically know more about themselves. Western societies encourage people to learn about themselves by

または、以下のようなコメントもいいでしょう。

「達成感があるでしょう／その人（子）の功績に感動しているで
しょう」
「私も行きたかったなぁ」

欧米人の多くは、話し手やその人の経験に興味を示す質問やコ
メントを喜びます。そしてもちろん、スモールトークに貢献でき
たことで、あなたにとってもよいPRになります。

スモールトークの準備

大いに「自己発見」に努めてください。私も含め日本人は、自分
が何を信じているのか、何を人生の原則としているのか、物事へ
の取り組み方などについて、常にはっきりと認識しているわけで
はありません。私たち日本人は、常に変化しつつある環境や状況に、
必要に応じて適応しなければならないと考えています。また、職
場や家庭で役割を果たすことのほうが、個人としての自分の在り
方よりも大切だと思いがちです。しかし、欧米人の多くは、個人
の人となりは、たまたま遭遇した状況に関係なく、一貫性があっ
て一定しているものだと信じています。その結果、もしあなたが
「ちょっとわかりません」や「状況によりますね」と答える回数が
多すぎると、あなたには人としての軸がないと思われてしまいま
す。これは、よいPRではありません。

欧米人はたいてい、自分のことをよく知っています。欧米社会
では、「どう思いますか？」「どうしてそのように考えるのです

147

constantly asking questions like, "What do you think?" "Why do you think so?" "What do you want to do?" "Which do you prefer?" Not surprisingly, they can answer these questions fairly quickly, because they have been asked those types of questions since they started talking as a child.

So, the best preparation for small talk is to learn about yourself. Ask yourself simple questions like, "Why do I like watching baseball?" "Why do I like this idea and not the other one?" "Why did I feel uncomfortable in a certain situation?" And try to come up with your individual/personal answers. In other words, "I felt exhilarated when I hit the ball the first time, and I wanted to feel it again and again," is a better answer than "Everybody played baseball when I grew up." Try to come up with answers that are not about the environment or situation (everybody played), but about your personal experience, beliefs, or feelings (I felt exhilarated). Small talk is a great way to connect with others on an individual level—person to person.

Additional points regarding small talk

Japanese tend to think in a negative form. This is because we want to avoid risks in general. And if you translate your Japanese thoughts into English, your message tends to lose some strength. For example, we would likely say in Japanese, "I always keep an umbrella with me so that I won't get wet

か?」「どうしたいですか?」「どちらが好きですか?」といった質問をくり返し尋ねられるので、自己発見しやすい環境にいるのです。言葉を話し始めたごく小さいころから、くり返し聞いてきたこのような質問に、欧米人がさっと答えることができるのも、納得できます。

　ですから、一番よいスモールトークの準備は、自己発見です。「どうして私は野球が好きなんだろう?」「どうして他のではなく、このアイデアが好きなんだろう?」「どうしてあの状況で居心地悪く感じたんだろう?」など、自問してみてください。そして、個人的な／自分なりの答えを見つけてください。言い換えれば、「最初にボールを打ったとき、ものすごく爽快だったので、同じ気持ちを何度も味わいたかったんです」の方が、「子どものころ、周りのみんなが野球をしていたから」より、欧米人にとってわかりやすい返答です。環境や状況(みんながやっていた)ではなく、ご自分の経験や信条、気持ち(爽快だった)から答えを引き出してください。スモールトークは、人間どうしの関係を築くのにとても役立ちます。

追加の留意点

　日本人は、否定形で考えがちです。これは、私たちがリスクを避けたいからです。あなたの日本的な考えをそのまま英語に訳すと、メッセージが萎えてしまいます。たとえば、私たちは日本語で「雨が降っても濡れないように、いつも傘を持ち歩いています」と言います。けれども英語で話すときは、同じ内容をよりポジ

if it rains." When you speak in English, though, you need to convert that statement into a more positive or cheerful mode: "I'm always prepared for rain because I keep an umbrella in my bag." I once read an article that recommended avoiding the phrase, "Be careful not to fall." The writer said that a negative sentence (in meaning) can give others a negative image and that can create negative consequences. I'm not sure if this is true or not; however, it is helpful to remember that most Westerners want to see things in a positive light. Remember, small talk is for your good PR, so it doesn't hurt to put a positive spin on what you are going to say.

When to have small talk at work

When to talk is also culturally defined. This is particularly challenging at work. When we have a conversation in Japan, we tend to have it after work, as we are busy taking care of our customers or important tasks during the work hours. However, most Westerners see developing working relationships as an activity that should take place during work hours. So, when you are set to have a conversation around 6:30 pm, all the Westerner colleagues may have already gone home. So be sure to make time for small talk during the work hours. You need an audience for your good PR!

Let's say you've run out of small talk topics, as you see the same people all the time. If you see a photo of his/her family

ティブで明るいモードに変更して、「傘をバッグに入れているので、いつでも雨に対する備えができています」と言ったほうがよいのです。一度、「転ばないように気をつけてね」と言わないほうがよいと書いてある記事を読んだことがあります。その筆者が言うには、（意味が）否定的な文章は、否定的なイメージを人に与え、否定的な結果を招きやすいというのです。これに信ぴょう性があるかどうかはわかりません。しかし、ほとんどの欧米人は、物事を肯定的に見たがっているということは覚えておいてください。スモールトークの目的はよいPRですから、言いたいことを肯定的に表現して損はありません。

職場でスモールトークをするタイミング

　世間話のタイミングは、文化によって違います。この差が、特に職場でややこしい問題となります。正規の就業時間中はお客さん対応や重要な作業で忙しいので、対話をするのは、往々にして仕事が終わった後です。しかし欧米人の多くは、職場での人間関係を築くのも、就業時間内に行う活動と考えています。あなたが夕方の6時半に話をしようと思ったとき、欧米人の同僚はみな帰宅してしまった後かもしれません。ですから、就業時間内に、スモールトークをする時間を作るようにしてください。聴いてくれる人がいなければ、よいPRも効果がありません。

　毎日同じ人に会うので、スモールトークの話題が尽きてしまったとしましょう。そんなとき、もしその人の家族やペットの写真

or pets, please ask about them. Although life in the office seems mundane and life-less sometimes, people are always doing something new or things change in our lives. If you see a picture drawn by his/her children or relatives, make a comment on them. Or when you see something interesting on his/her screensaver, ask about it.

Privacy issues

When you see souvenirs, photos, or other artifacts on someone's desk, please take that as an invitation for small talk. These are the cues telling you, "I'm happy to talk about these things." However, as we discussed above (Topics to avoid talking about), please avoid questions that are considered to be "private." Let's say you see your colleague in a picture when she was younger, and she explains that she was in college at that time. Please avoid asking questions like, "How many years ago was that?" Also avoid saying something like, "You look much younger in that photo." Instead, ask where they were in the picture and what they were doing so that she can share her experience with you. "What a nice picture! Was that a family gathering?" "I see mountains in the background. Did you go hiking?"

Hobbies

What is your answer to the question, "What is your hobby?" If it is "eating gourmet food," or "I'm a food buff," I'd like you to reconsider that response. Here's why.

を見かけたら、質問をしてください。職場で過ごす時間は決まりきっていて面白味がないと思うときもありますが、人はいつも何か新しいことをしていて、生活にも変化があります。同僚の子どもや親せきが描いた絵を見たら、何かコメントをしてください。誰かのスクリーンセーバーに面白いものが出ていたら、質問してみてください。

プライバシーについて

　誰かの机の上にお土産や写真、その他の品物を見たら、スモールトークへの誘いだと思ってください。持ち主からの「これらについて、喜んで話しますよ」という合図なのです。しかし、上述したように（p.139「避けるべき話題」）、「プライバシーに関する」話題は、避けるようにしてください。たとえば、女性の同僚が若かったときの写真を見たとき、彼女が大学のときの写真だと説明したとします。「それって、何年前？」のような質問は避けてください。また、「ずいぶん若く見えるねぇ」などと言うのもいただけません。そのかわりに、「どこで撮った写真なのか」「何をしたのか」など、彼女が自分の経験を披露できるような質問をしてください。「いい写真ですねぇ。家族の集まりだったんですか？」「背景に山が見えますね。ハイキングに行かれたんですか？」などと尋ねるのがよいでしょう。

趣味

　「あなたの趣味は何ですか？」という質問に対し、どう答えますか？　もしそれが、「食道楽です」「おいしいものに目がありません」の類であれば、再検討をお願いします。

153

According to the Oxford Dictionary of English, a hobby is "an activity done regularly in one's leisure time for pleasure." The Collins COBUILD Advanced Dictionary of English says, "A hobby is an activity that you enjoy doing in your spare time." The common denominator is "activity." The word "activity" is derived from the adjective "active." And eating food, gourmet or not, isn't seen as a noteworthy activity in the English-speaking world. Sure, you can argue that eating is an activity, however, it's more passive than active. It is something you do to sustain your life, like sleeping. You can have a good, long, dreamful, or energizing sleep, but it's still something you have to do to keep living.

So, I'd like you to think of ways to tweak "My hobby is eating good food" so that you can make it more "active." Here are some of my suggestions:

"I'm creating a review of ramen noodles in Fukuoka. Please feel free to ask me about any of the ramen shops. I'm happy to share my thoughts on them."

"My hobby is cooking. I go to all sorts of gourmet restaurants and then try to make similar dishes at home with ingredients that I can find at my local supermarket."

"I enjoy experiencing Japanese local food culture. On weekends, I often travel to a place where I've never been to, and find something interesting to eat. Japan is a small country that offers a great diversity of seafood and vegetables."

"I love throwing small parties with small dishes, tapas style. It's fun to get together and chat over drinks and

オックスフォード英英辞典によると、趣味とは「自分の時間に楽しみのために定期的にする活動」です。コリンズ・コウビルド英英辞典によると、「趣味は余暇に楽しむ活動」です。両者の趣味の定義に共通しているのは、「活動」です。英語の「活動（activity）」と言う言葉は、形容詞「active」から派生したものです。食事をとるのは、グルメフードかどうかに関わらず、英語圏では特筆するに足らない活動なのです。食べることは活動の一種だと主張されるかもしれませんが、それはどちらかというと受け身な動作です。睡眠と同じように、生きるためにすることです。ぐっすりと長く眠り、夢をたくさん見たかもしれませんし、精気が戻ったかもしれません、でも、睡眠は生きるためにすることだということに変わりはありません。

　ですから、「私の趣味はおいしいものを食べることです」という発言をひねって、もっと「活動的」に聞こえる方法を考えてみましょう。以下をご参照ください。

　　「福岡のラーメン比較をしています。ラーメン屋について質問があったら、どうぞ遠慮なく聞いてください。私の考えを喜んで話します」

　　「私の趣味は料理です。いろんなグルメのレストランに出かけ、その後、近所のスーパーで買える材料で似たような料理を作ります」

　　「日本の地方の食文化を経験するのが楽しいです。週末に、行ったことのない所へ旅行し、面白い食べ物を見つけます。日本は小さい国ですが、海鮮料理と野菜料理の多様性はすばらしいです」

　　「タパススタイルで小皿料理のパーティーをするのが大好きです。集まって、飲んだり食べたりしながら談笑するのは楽

food. Actually, I'm having another one this weekend. Would you like to join us?"

If your gourmet eating is only about eating, then I suggest that you find something else to share as your hobby. Just "eating good food," even if it gives you enormous pleasure, sounds as if you have no other pleasure in life, or no friends to share good food with, or you have no interest in the world. Either way, it's poor PR.

❖ Summary ❖

You can use small talk for your good PR.

To make your small talk a success, keep it upbeat and short.

しいものです。実は、今週末もパーティーをします。よかったら、来ませんか？」

　もしあなたのグルメの趣味が食べるだけだったら、別のものを趣味として話してはいかがでしょうか？「おいしいものを食べる」ことで、とてつもない喜びを得ているとしても、人生に他の喜びがないかのように、または、おいしいものを一緒に食べる友だちがいないかのように、さらには、世の中に全く興味がないかのように聞こえてしまいます。いずれにしても、PRとしては逆効果です。

❖ まとめ ❖

スモールトークは自己PRのツール。

元気に短く話すのが、スモールトーク成功のコツ。

Let's try the following:

Practice introducing yourself in 30 seconds. These are some examples of topics.

· Hobby (preferably talk about something other than eating good food).

· Select topics that you'd like others to know, e.g. your family, pet, your neighborhood, some noteworthy events.

· Talk about something you do in your daily life, and why you do it. For example, you walk up and down the stairs instead of using the elevators for your health.

· Volunteer activities that you do to contribute to society. (For Westerners, a volunteer activity is an opportunity to express their own values.)

· Your foibles that you can share and laugh about.

やってみよう

30秒で自己紹介する練習を。以下は話題の例。

・趣味（できればグルメ以外）

・家族やペット、近所の様子、ちょっとした出来事など、周囲
　の人に知ってもらいたい内容を選択

・日常的にしていることについて、理由を含めて説明。たとえ
　ば、健康のためにエレベーターを使わずに階段を上り下りし
　ているなど。

・ボランティア活動などの社会貢献（欧米人にとって、ボラン
　ティア活動は個人の価値観を表現する一つの方法）

・笑える失敗談

Chapter IV

How to Have a Good Conversation

"Conversation" we'll talk about in this book

First, let's have a conversation about conversations. Sometimes it's hard to find a single perfect Japanese translation for an English word. "Conversation" is one of those words. It can be 会話、談話、座談、対談、非公式交渉、親交、and so on. So, let's first discuss what a conversation is.

The Oxford Dictionary defines it as "A talk, especially an informal one, between two or more people, in which news and ideas are exchanged." Collins COBUILD says, "If you have a conversation with someone, you talk with them, usually in an informal situation." The Oxford Thesaurus of English lists "discussion" as the first synonym. I'd like to define "conversation" in this book in three parts:

1. Communication is two-way

2. Communication is informal in most cases

第4章

対話を通じて理解を深める

この本で話す「対話」の定義

　まず、conversations について話しましょう。英語の単語にぴったりくる日本語を見つけるのが難しいことがあります。「Conversation」もその一つです。会話、談話、座談、対談、非公式交渉、親交など、いろんな訳が思い浮かびます。ですから、まず最初に、ここでの conversation が何かを議論しましょう。

　オックスフォード英英辞典は、「通常形式ばらない、二人以上の人数で行う会話で、ニュースやアイデアを交換するためのもの」とし、コウビルド英英辞典は、「誰かと conversation をするとき、通常、気楽な状況で話す」とあります。オックスフォード類語辞典には、discussion が最初の同義語に挙げられています。本書では、conversation を以下の三つで定義したいと思います。

1. 双方向のコミュニケーション
2. ほとんどの場合、形式ばらないコミュニケーション

3. The communication creates an environment where participants exchange their news and ideas

Communication is two-way

This may seem obvious; however, Japanese have a reputation that they usually talk very little at first, and then talk too much or too long once they start talking. So, in order to make the communication two-way, we need to be cognizant of a few things.

- Think of conversation as a game of catch. You receive the ball, keep it for a while, and then throw it to someone else. If you're responding to a question, keep your responses short (thirty seconds or so), and then ask the inquirer or other conversation partners for their input.

- When you want to catch the conversation ball, make that clear with a hand gesture, or leaning forward, or saying something like, "Well," or "I know what you mean … "

Communication is informal in most cases

So, if two lawyers exchange opposing ideas in court, even though the communication may be two-way, we don't call it a

3. コミュニケーションによって参加者どうしがニュースとアイデア、意見を交換する環境が生まれる

■対話の定義［1］
双方向のコミュニケーション

　これは、当たり前のことに思えるかもしれません。しかし、日本人は、最初はほとんどしゃべらず、その後いったん話し出すと、話が広がりすぎる、もしくは長く話しすぎると言われます。ですから、コミュニケーションが双方向であるようにするには、以下の点に注意する必要があります。

・対話（conversation）をキャッチボールと考えること。ボールを受け取り、しばらくボールを持ち続けた後、誰かに投げます。質問に答えている場合は、返答を短くし（約30秒）、質問者や他の人に意見や情報を求めます。

・対話のボールを受け取りたいときは、手の動きや、前に身を乗り出したり、「そうだなぁ、（Well, ...）」「言っていること、わかるよ（I know what you mean）」と言うなどして、その意志を明確に伝える。

■対話の定義［2］
ほとんどの場合、形式ばらないコミュニケーション

　ですから、裁判所で二人の弁護士が相反する意見を交換しても、確かにコミュニケーションは双方向ですが、正式なものなの

conversation, as it's very formal. However, a real conversation between them may happen outside of court.

Exchanging news and ideas can take place in small talk. However, the amount of information we exchange in small talk is usually limited, as the focus is to project a positive image of ourselves and to check everyone else's pulse and confirm, "We're good to go today."

In conversations, we can share more detailed information, inspire and learn from each other, and also make decisions together.

So, for the purpose of this chapter, I'd like to define "conversation" as a two-way informal communication where news, ideas and opinions are exchanged.

Preparation for a good conversation in English

So, how can you have a good conversation in English? Even if you're fluent in English, that alone doesn't guarantee a good conversation. You need to show the following to your conversation partner(s). And what you do physically can play a bigger role than your English language skills. In Intercultural Communication, the field that I work in, this is called

で、それを対話とは呼びません。しかし、裁判所の外では、この弁護士たちも本当の対話をする可能性があります。

■ 対話の定義 [3]

コミュニケーションによって、参加者どうしがニュースとアイデア、意見を交換する環境が生まれる

スモールトークでもニュースやアイデアの交換をします。しかしスモールトークの目的は、自分のポジティブなイメージを投影したり、その場の人たちの調子を確かめたり、また「みんな今日も元気だ」というのを確認することなので、交換する情報の量は限られます。

対話では、より詳細な情報を共有し、お互いによい刺激を与えたり学んだりし、また、一緒に意思決定を行ったりします。

ですから、この章では対話を「双方向の形式ばらないコミュニケーションで、ニュースやアイデア、意見を交換するもの」と定義します。

英語で対話をする準備

では、どうしたら英語で対話する準備ができるのでしょうか？英語が流暢でも、それだけでよい対話になる保証はありません。以下のことを、対話の相手に示す必要があります。また、英語のスキルよりも、体で表現することが対話の出来不出来を大きく左右します。異文化コミュニケーションという、私が働く分野では、これを「非言語コミュニケーション」と呼びます。

"nonverbal communication."

Ways to show that you're engaged in the conversation

How do you show that you're engaged in the conversation? The following are some nonverbal communication skills that you can use:

● Sustained eye contact

Eye contact plays a big role in English communication. If you have sustained eye contact, your conversation partners will understand that you're interested in them as well as the topics/subjects. So, how long do you have to maintain eye contact? I'd recommend five seconds. Younger generations in Japan tend to have long enough eye contact; however, I have also met many young Japanese who will look in another direction after three seconds. Three seconds isn't long enough to demonstrate your interest. If your eye contact is too short, your conversation partners may interpret that in a way that you didn't mean, like the following:

You're not interested in having a conversation

You're not interested in the topic/subject

You may not be interested in your conversation partners

You aren't friendly or don't care about other people

対話に熱心に参加していることを示す方法

　対話に積極的に参加していることをどうやって表現しますか？ 以下は、使っていただきたい非言語コミュニケーションのスキルです。

● 相手の目をじっとみる

　欧米人との英語のコミュニケーションでは、相手と視線を合わせられるかどうかが、対話の成功に大きく関わってきます。相手と視線を合わせることができれば、あなたが話題や案件だけでなく、対話の相手にも興味を持っていると理解してもらえます。どれぐらいの間、相手と目を合わせればよいのでしょうか？ 私のおすすめは５秒間です。若い世代の日本人は、十分長く相手の目を見ていられる人が多いです。しかし、３秒経つと視線をずらしてしまう人もたくさんいます。３秒では、あなたの興味を示すには短すぎます。視線を合わせている時間が短すぎると、相手は、以下のように、思いもよらない方向に解釈してしまうことがあります。

　　対話を持つことに興味がない

　　話題や案件に興味がない

　　対話の相手に興味がない

　　愛想がない、または他人に関心がない

You don't have your own opinions

You're not confident

You're hiding something

You're not an honest person

The list goes on and on, and it won't ever go in a positive direction. In other words, if you want to let them know that you're engaged in the conversation, then you need to keep eye contact for five seconds or longer.

● Open posture

I'm talking about physical posture here and not mental attitude. Open posture is a relaxed posture, sometimes leaning forward. This is not an Asian's typical posture during a conversation. Many of us tend to fold our arms when we have a conversation. This is an Asian's way of telling others that we're interested in the subject. However, in the Western world, this is considered a "closed posture," which suggests that you're not willing to listen to others' ideas or opinions. Folding one's arms suggests a "my way or the highway" attitude, and is not conducive to a good conversation.

If you're standing, use some hand motions and show that you're excited and eager to listen and speak. If you're sitting in a chair, you can lean back a little in order to show your openness and confidence. You can lean forward when you're really interested in the subject.

あなたには自分の意見がない

　　あなたは自信のない人だ

　　あなたは何かを隠している

　　あなたは正直ではない

　リストはまだまだ続きますが、けっしてよい方向へ転換しません。ですから、あなたが対話に熱心に参加していることを伝えるには、まず相手の目を見ること、そして一度目を合わせたら少なくとも5秒は視線を逸らさないことが必要です。

● 開放的な姿勢

　ここで話しているのは、体の姿勢であって、心的な態度ではありません。開放的な姿勢とは、くつろいだ姿勢で、前に乗り出していることもあります。これは、アジア人が対話をするときの典型的な姿勢ではありません。私たちは、対話中に腕を組むことが多いです。これはアジアでは、話の内容に興味を示す一つの方法です。しかし欧米では、「閉じた姿勢」とされ、相手のアイデアや意見を積極的に聞くつもりがないことを示唆します。腕を組んだ姿勢は、「私の意見通りにならなければ気がすまない」という態度を暗に示し、よい対話の雰囲気を損ねてしまいます。

　立っている場合は、手の動きを使って、あなたがワクワクしていること、聞いたり話したりしたいということを示しましょう。椅子に座っているなら、相手の意見を受け入れる用意があることや、自信があることを示すために、少し後ろにもたれるのもいいでしょう。話の内容にすごく興味があるときは、前に身を乗り出してみてください。

● Nodding

Nodding accompanied by "uh-huh" shows that you're listening and want to hear more. Be sure to say "uh-huh" with a rising tone. If you say "uh-huh" with a falling tone, it means "no." Mixing "uh-huh" (rising tone) with an occasional "I see," "that's interesting," "that sounds great," or any other short expressions will make the conversation more natural. Try not to say "uh-huh" too often though, especially on a call, as too many "uh-huhs" can break the rhythm of the speaker and make it difficult for others to hear the speaker.

■ Nonverbal Communication Skills [2]

Curiosity

● Be curious!

Curiosity can come from your experiences in life, although it can also come from a lack of them. In general, having a little bit of experience in a topic can make you more curious about it. My observation is that people outside of Japan have a wider range of experiences in their lives, simply because that is encouraged by their society. Although volunteering, for example, is becoming more common in Japan, it is not encouraged as much as it is in other countries. Many Japanese children also go to *juku* or a cramming school instead of playing sports. However, most high school students in the U.S., for example, play sports or take art or music lessons, volunteer, and earn money as well

● 頷く

「アハ↗（「ハ」で音を上げる）」と言いながら頷くと、あなたは耳を傾けていて、もっと聞きたいと思っていることを示せます。「アハ↗」と上向きに言うようにしてください。もし音をハで下げるように言うと、「ノー」の意味になります。「アハ↗」に、ときどき「なるほど」や「面白いね」「すごいね」などその他の短い表現を入れると、より自然な対話になります。ただし、「アハ↗」をあまり頻繁に言いすぎてはいけません。特に電話会議では、これを言いすぎると話し手のリズムを崩し、他の人が話を聞きにくくなってしまいます。

■非言語コミュニケーションスキル［2］
好奇心

● 興味を持とう！

　好奇心は、経験していないことに対して持つこともありますが、人生で経験したことの中から湧いてくることが多いものです。一般に、話題になっていることを少し経験したことがあると、もっと興味が湧くものです。私の見たところ、日本以外の場所で暮らす人たちは、彼らの住む社会に背中を押される形で、広い人生経験を持つようになります。ボランティア活動は日本でも一般化しつつありますが、それでも他の国に比べれば、追い風が吹いているとは言えません。日本の子どもたちの多くは、スポーツをせず、塾に通います。けれども、たとえばアメリカのほとんどの学生は、勉強をするかたわらスポーツをしたり、美術や音楽のレッスンを受けたり、ボランティア活動をしたり、お金を稼い

171

as study. They have broader experiences in life and are more curious about many things in life. This makes them better at having conversations. So, I'd like to ask you to become more curious about more things than you have been in the past. And no matter what the subject is, try to listen to the speaker intently, and if you can, please ask questions.

● Be aware of your nonverbal messages

Most Japanese are too polite to say, "I'm not interested." But for the sake of argument, let's say you did say that to your conversation partners. The conversation will stop right there rather awkwardly. Or you'll be excluded from the conversation even if you're there physically.

The tricky part is nonverbals. Your nonverbals, like eye contact, tone of voice, posture, and so on, can reveal or betray you. Your nonverbals may reveal your lack of interest inadvertently, even though you didn't express it in words. Or when you're really interested, your nonverbals may be sending the wrong message: I'm not interested. So, please be aware of your nonverbal messages in a conversation.

● Respond positively to differences

This is a generalization and doesn't apply to every Japanese; however, we tend to become less interested in others and their opinions when we perceive differences between the speaker

だりします。彼らは広い経験があり、いろんなことに興味があります。このため、彼らは対話に長けているのです。ですから、今までよりもっと多くのことに、より興味を持っていただきたいのです。そして、話の内容が何であれ、相手の話に一生懸命耳を傾け、質問をするように心がけてください。

● 非言語メッセージに気をつけよう

　日本人は相手のことを思いやるので、「興味がありません」と言う人はなかなかいません。しかし、ここで仮に相手にそう言ってしまったとしましょう。すると、その場で居心地の悪さを残したまま、対話は終わってしまいます。もしくは、あなたがまだその場にいても、他の人たちだけで対話が進むでしょう。

　ややこしいのは、非言語コミュニケーションです。視線や声音、姿勢などが、あなたの本心をさらけ出してしまったり、本心と違うメッセージを送ってしまったりします。言葉で表現しなくても、興味がないことを、あなたの非言語コミュニケーションが、ついばらしてしまうかもしれません。もしくは、本当は興味があるのに、あなたの非言語コミュニケーションは、「興味がない」という本心とは裏腹のメッセージを送っているかもしれません。ですから、対話中の非言語メッセージに注意を払うようにしてください。

● 違いに前向きに対応

　これは一般化した議論で、日本人全員に当てはまるわけではありませんが、私たちは相手との違いに気がつくと、その人やその人の意見への興味が萎えてしまいがちです。これは、私たちが自

and ourselves. This is because we're accustomed to speaking with someone like us. In Japan, we make and maintain connections with others through similarities, and tend not to pay the same level of attention to someone whose opinions are different.

This tendency is also expressed in Japanese language. When we say in Japanese "she's different," it could mean "she is wrong" or "she is strange." We don't have a positive image about being different.

On the other hand, in most Western countries—especially immigrant countries like the U.S., Canada, and Australia where many people with many different backgrounds live together—people are more interested in differences. In fact, they don't think they need to talk to each other if they agree on everything. They're interested in exchanging different views and ideas. Being different can be a very good thing, especially when it comes to conversations. For the same reason, being new can also be a positive thing.

In Japan, we tend to be attracted to and communicate with people that we feel we have much in common. But I'd like you to take on a new attitude when you communicate with non-Japanese. Try to make connections with non-Japanese through some of the similarities you can find. This is easier said than done.

Most non-Japanese are interested in differences and usually don't need to have much in common with anyone to start a

分と似た人と話すことに慣れているからです。日本人は共通点を通じて人間関係を築き、つき合います。そして、意見が違う人にはあまり注意を払いません。

　この傾向は、日本語にも表現されています。日本語で「彼女、違うよね」と言うとき、「彼女は間違っている」または「彼女、変だよね」という意味のことがあります。私たちは「違う」ということに対してあまりいい印象を持っていないのです。

　一方、多くの欧米諸国、特に移民が多く、生い立ちの違う人がたくさん住むアメリカ、カナダ、オーストラリアの人たちは、違いにこそ興味があります。実際、彼らはすべての点に合意できるのであれば、話す必要はないと考えます。彼らは、違った見方やアイデアの交換に興味があります。人と違うことはよいことで、特に対話では、その違いが興味をそそることになります。同じ理由で、新しいものごとも、対話に役立ちます。

　日本では、共通点がかなりあると感じる人に惹かれ、話すことが多いです。けれども海外の人と話す場合は、今までとは違う姿勢で接していただきたいのです。海外の人とは、何らかの共通点を見つけて、人間関係を築く努力をしてみてください。これは、言うのは簡単ですが、実行するのはそう簡単ではありません。

　海外の人は違いに興味があり、たいして共通点がない人とでも対話を始めます。そういう彼らからすると、日本人があたかも見

conversation. Sometimes they feel as if Japanese are putting up invisible barriers and refusing to have a conversation. Of course, most of us don't mean that, it's just that we don't feel comfortable speaking with someone we don't know much about. But without talking with them, how can we know about them? See, it's a chicken-and-egg problem. We need to somehow overcome this initial discomfort.

For example, I have heard a Japanese say, "I can't be her friend, as she doesn't have kids." But, both of them are women, and that similarity can cover half of the world's population. Try not to add many "conditions" to your conversation partners. Once you speak with someone you think is different, you may discover that these differences are not critical. You may even come to enjoy the differences.

Many times, I also have heard Japanese say, "My colleague and I have different views on this." The people making that statement seem to be disappointed and discouraged to talk with his/her colleague. But again, the fact that you both work for the same company and share some common business goals will mean that you have something in common. My point is that I'd like you to find something that you have in common with others and encourage yourself to speak with them, even when you feel discouraged about speaking with them. If you do, you may be surprised in a good way! And I hope that you practice the same with your fellow Japanese. We have so much to learn from each other.

えない壁を作り、対話を拒否しているように感じられることがあります。もちろん、日本人にはそういうつもりはなく、ただ、あまりよく知らない人と話すのを気詰まりに感じているだけです。けれども、海外の人と話すことなく、どうやって彼らのことを知ることができるのでしょうか？ これは、鶏が先か卵が先か、の問題と同じです。私たちはどうにかして、この最初の居心地の悪さを克服しなければなりません。

　たとえば、「私は彼女と友だちにはなれないわ。だって、彼女には子どもがいないから」と言う人がいます。けれども、二人とも女性で、この共通点は世界の人口の半分です。どうか、あまりたくさんの「条件」を、対話相手の選択基準に加えないでください。共通点がないと思っていた相手と話してみたら、違いはたいして重要ではないことに気づくかもしれません。そればかりか、違いを楽しめるようになるかもしれません。

　また、日本人が「この点についてアメリカ人の同僚と意見が合わない」と言うのも、何度も耳にしました。その人たちはがっかりし、同僚と話す気になれないようでした。けれども、あなたは同僚と同じ会社で働き、共通のビジネス・ゴールをいくつか掲げているのですから、同僚との間に共通点を持っているはずです。私が言いたいのは、たとえ内心では相手と話しにくいと感じていても、共通点を見つけ、その人たちと進んで話してくださいということです。話してみれば、意外と楽しい発見があるかもしれません。そして同じことを、日本人どうしの中でも実践していただきたいのです。お互いから学べることが、たくさんあるのですから。

● Make a positive comment and then ask a question

Then, how do you show that you're interested and/or curious? By asking questions! However, asking questions continuously may be counter-productive, as your conversation partners may feel as if they're being interrogated. An interrogation isn't a conversation, as it is neither two-way nor informal. So, I recommend making a positive comment and then asking a follow-up question. Remember something or someone being different or new can be positive.

Path to Mastery 12

Examples of the "positive comment + question" pattern

"I like your sweater. Can you tell me where you bought it?"

"Your sneakers look great! I've never seen sneakers in that color. Do you mind sharing where you bought them?"

"Your lunch looks delicious. Did you get it somewhere new?"

"I've never been to Brazil. Can you tell me what it's like there?"

"I've never thought about it that way. Can you tell me more?"

"How interesting! That is a new way of looking at it. Would you mind explaining why you see it that way?"

● 肯定的なコメントを述べて、質問する

　では、どうすれば、あなたが興味がある、または好奇心がある
ことを伝えられるのでしょう？ 質問をするのです！ しかし、立
て続けに質問をするのは、逆効果です。相手は職務質問をされて
いるように感じるかもしれません。質問は双方向でもくつろいだ
コミュニケーションでもないので、対話ではありません。ですか
ら、肯定的なコメントをした後に、関連の質問することをおすす
めします。人や物事に違う点や新しい点がある場合、英語の対話
では前向きに評価されることを覚えておいてください。

＋ コミュニケーションの極意 12　[肯定的なコメントを言う]

　肯定的なコメント＋質問の例

　「そのセーターいいね。どこで買ったか教えてくれる？」

　「そのスニーカー、かっこいいね。見たことない色だよ。ど
　こで買ったか教えてくれる？」

　「おいしそうなお弁当だね。どこか新しいところで買った
　の？」

　「ブラジルに行ったことないんだ。どんな風なのか、話して
　くれる？」

　「そんな風に考えたことないよ。それについて、もっと話し
　てくれる？」

　「面白いねぇ！ 新しい見方だね。どうしてそんな風に考える
　のか、説明してもらえる？」

Ways to get your conversation partners interested in your story

If your conversation partners show interest in your story, then you can elaborate on it. However, make sure to tell them the conclusion or the most impactful part first. Then, follow the "play catch" rule and invite their questions. If you can't tell them either of those parts first, then, I'd suggest a third option.

● Problem-solving mode

If you're going to tell others the story of *The Peach Boy* (Momotaro in Japanese), how are you going to tell it in English? What are you going to mention first? I guarantee you that you'll lose your audience if you start by telling how Momotaro was born. *Tasty Baby Belly Buttons* by Judy Sierra tells in English a version of Momotaro that comes from Shimane Prefecture. The story is the same but the protagonist is a girl. The first sentence of her book is "In Japan, long ago, many towns and villages were terrorized by a gang of *oni*." When you can't give your conversation partners the conclusion or the most exciting part first, then begin with the problem that you're going to solve.

Capacity to suspend judgment

When I explain Japanese culture to non-Japanese, I

あなたの話に興味を持ってもらうには

　相手があなたの話に興味を持ってくれたら、詳しく話してください。ただし、話の結論、もしくは一番印象に残る部分を先に話すようにします。その後、「キャッチボール」ルールに従って、質問を受けるようにします。結論や一番面白い点を先に話せない場合に備え、おすすめしたい三つ目の選択肢があります。

● 問題解決モード
　日本の昔話「桃太郎」の話をするとしたら、英語でどうやって物語を伝えますか？ 何について一番最初に話しますか？ 欧米人相手に、まず桃太郎の出生から話しはじめると、聞き手の誰もが興味をなくしてしまうこと、請け合いです。ジュディ・シエラという作者が書いた Tasty Baby Belly Buttons は、島根県に伝えられている桃太郎の話です。話の筋はおなじみの「桃太郎」ですが、主人公は女の子です。この本の最初の文は、「昔むかし日本には、鬼に荒らされた町や村がたくさんありました」です。結論や一番面白いところを最初に話せない場合、このようにこれから解決する（すべき）問題から話し出すのも一つの手です。

判断を保留する能力

　日本の文化を海外の人に説明するとき、私は物事の一定のやり

explain *kata*, or set ways of doing things. The fact that we have so many art forms that comes with "*do*" (道), like *judo*, *kado* (flower arrangement), *sado* (tea ceremony), and *shodo* (calligraphy) shows the Japanese propensity towards set ways. It never occurs to most people in other countries that they have to spend many years learning these art forms. They just arrange flowers in their own way. Who cares how they make their own cup of tea! But in Japan, these are praised as high forms of how to live well.

And this is not limited to art form. This hits home when I talk with my Japanese friends—mostly women. They can have an animated conversation about how to keep white socks white by pre-washing them by hand and then putting them in the laundry machine. And then they can vigorously debate the features of different laundry machines. Me? I just give my kids colored socks, so that stains will be less obvious.

In business, too, we create and follow set ways. New employees in a Japanese company will learn how to create documents in their company's specific way. Japanese tend to work for the same company for a long time, so getting used to a certain way of doing things within the company makes their work life more efficient and comfortable.

Let's say you've worked for a Japanese company in Japan for more than eight years, and you probably know how to do things according to that company's way—what is accepted and what is not. Then, if you're transferred to the New York

方、「型」について説明します。柔道や華道、茶道、書道のように「道」がつく芸術が多くあるのは、日本人の決まったやり方への志向を表しています。このように何年も費やして芸術を学ぶというのは、他の国の人たちには思いもよらないことです。彼らは自分の好きなように花を生けます。自分のお茶をどう淹れようと、誰がかまうものですか！ しかし日本では、これらの芸術は、高尚な生活の型として賞賛されています。

そしてこれは、芸術に限ったことではありません。日本人の友だち（ほとんどは女性）と話すとき、しみじみと感じます。たとえば、白いソックスをまず手洗いしてから洗濯機で洗うことで白さを保つことについて、活発に話し合います。その後、いろいろな洗濯機の機能についてあれこれと討論します。私？ 我が家の子どもには、シミが目立たない色つきのソックスを買っています。

ビジネスでも、一定のやり方を作り、それを守るのが日本です。日本の新入社員は、それぞれが勤める企業の文書作成方法を学びます。日本では同じ会社で長く働く人が多いので、企業内での物事の進め方を学ぶことで、仕事の効率が上がり、やりやすくなるのです。

日本の企業で8年以上働くと、その会社での仕事のしかた、つまり、何が受け入れられ、何が受け入れられないかがわかってきます。その後、ニューヨーク支店に異動になり、アメリカ人の仕事のしかたを目の当たりにしたとします。おそらく、びっくりす

branch, you'll encounter American employees' ways of doing things. Most likely you will be surprised or possibly even upset about it. Then, you'll probably judge them or their way of doing things as "inferior."

Right then and there, I'd like you to suspend judgment. Assume that they have their reasons for their ways, and encourage yourself to become curious. And ask questions like,

"Can you tell me why you chose this format?"

"Have you thought about other options?"

"What works best for you with this format?"

And learn their reasons for their ways. Judging immediately good/bad, or right/wrong doesn't guide you to a better place. Make sure the conversation is two-way, and that you're projecting your openness through words and nonverbal messages.

How to have a good conversation in English

Okay, now you have a basic knowledge about how to have a good conversation. Let's talk about actual English sentences that we can use in conversations.

■ Try These in Your English Conversation [1]
Open-ended questions

There are two kinds of questions: closed questions and

るでしょうし、ムッとすることもあるでしょう。そして、アメリカ人や彼らの仕事のしかたを「劣っている」と判断するでしょう。

　その時点で、判断を保留してもらいたいのです。彼らには彼らなりの理由があることを前提に、好奇心を持つ努力をしてください。そして、以下のような質問をしてみてください。

　「どうしてこのフォーマットを使うことにしたのか、教えてもらえますか？」

　「他の選択肢について、考えてみましたか？」

　「このフォーマットの一番よい点は何ですか？」

　こうして、彼らの理由を学ぶのです。即座に善悪や正しいかどうかを判断してしまうと、状況の改善は望めません。双方向の対話と、言葉と非言語メッセージの両方で、あなたが相手の意見を聞く用意があることを示してください。

実のある対話を英語でするには

　ここまで読まれた方は、対話に必要な基本知識を得たことと思います。次に、実際の対話で使える英文について考えてみましょう。

■対話に使える英文［1］
自由回答を求める質問

　質問には、種類が二つあります。限定質問と自由回答質問です。

open-ended questions. Closed questions are questions that you answer with a "yes" or "no." To have a good conversation where you can exchange news and ideas, you need to ask more open-ended questions than closed questions. Please see below.

A: Do you like baseball?

B: Yes.

The conversation could end here if you asked a closed question. (Well, in reality, most Americans will keep talking.)

A: What kind of sports do you like?

B: I like tennis. Tennis involves moment-by-moment decision-making by players. You can also switch from defense to offense in an instant. It's such an exciting game!

You can see that open-ended questions are more inviting, and it becomes easier for your conversation partners to share what they feel or know about the subject. Here are some more examples of open-ended questions.

"How was your weekend?

"How do you like to spend your weekends?

"What are your plans for the summer/weekend?

"Where do you go for vacation?

限定質問には、「はい」か「いいえ」で答えます。ニュースやアイデアの交換ができる対話をするには、限定質問よりも自由回答質問を多くする必要があります。

　　A: 野球、好き？
　　B: はい。

　対話はここで終わってしまう可能性があります（もっとも実際には、ほとんどのアメリカ人はしゃべり続けます）。

　　A: どんなスポーツが好き？
　　B: 私はテニスが好きです。テニス選手は一瞬で意思決定をします。また、一瞬で守りから攻撃に転換することができます。ワクワクするゲームですよ！

　自由回答質問をすると、相手を対話に引き込むことができますし、その人が話題について感じていることや知っていることを話しやすくなります。以下は自由回答質問の例です。

「週末はどうでした？」

「週末はどうやって過ごすのが好き？」

|夏／週末の計画は？」

「休暇でどこに行くの？」

"Where did you grow up?

"What was it like growing up in China (or any other countries and places)?"

"What movies have you seen recently?"

"What TV shows do you watch?"

"Who is your favorite actor?"

"Who is your favorite author?"

"What is your favorite restaurant for lunch?"

"Where did you go to college? What was your major?"

"How is your day going?"

"What kind of music do you listen to?"

"Which country did you enjoy the most, for living or traveling?"

"What is on your bucket list?"

"How would you describe yourself?"

■ Try These in Your English Conversation [2]

Be ready to answer open-ended questions

In this chapter, we talk about the importance of two-way communication in conversations. So, you should not only ask open-ended questions, but also be ready to answer those questions. The worst answer you can give is "I'm not sure," because they don't learn anything about you. Are you not sure because you don't have any experience with it, or you're hesitant to say something, or you're not interested? So, even

「どこで育ったの？」

「中国（その他の国や場所）で育つのはどんな感じ？」

「最近見た映画は？」

「どのテレビ番組を見てるの？」

「どの俳優がすき？」

「どの著者が好き？」

「ランチに行くレストランで好きなのは？」

「どこの大学に行ったの？ 専攻は？」

「今日の調子はどう？」

「どんな音楽を聴くの？」

「住むのと旅行するのに、どの国が一番楽しかった？」

「生きているうちにやりたいことは？」

「自分のことをどう説明しますか？」

■対話に使える英文［2］
自由回答質問に答えるには

この章では、対話における双方向のコミュニケーションの大切さを話してきました。ですから、自由回答質問をするだけでなく、答える用意も必要です。最悪の返事は「ちょっとわかりません」です。これでは相手はあなたについて何も知ることができません。あなたがわからないのは、それについて経験がないからですか、それとも何かを言うのをためらっているのですか、または興味がないのでしょうか？ いろんな含みのある表現ですから、日本語で

when "you're not sure" in a Japanese sense, you need to be sure to say something.

"Well, I've never thought about it."

"That sounds interesting, but I've never done it before."

"You know, I have played it before, but it's just not my kind of sport."

"I used to swim once a week, but I got a very bad flu one year, and that was the end of swimming for me."

"I've never been to Africa. It is such an intriguing continent, but I don't know what to expect there."

"I know venison is a delicacy, but I feel a bit uncomfortable about eating deer."

Keep talking! (But not too long)

I touched on this subject at the beginning of this chapter (1. Communication is two-way). I'd like to elaborate further on two-way communication.

Let's say someone asked you a closed question:

A: Do you like traveling to other countries for vacation?

B: Yes.

Closed questions (yes/no questions) like this aren't inviting. However, you need to talk more, so that you can have a

「ちょっとわかりません」とぼかす場面でも、必ず何かを言うようにしてください。

　「えーっと、考えたことないです」

　「面白そうですが、やったことがないです」

　「実は、一度やったことがあるんですが、私にしっくりくるスポーツではないです」

　「週に一度泳いでいたこともありましたが、ある年ひどいインフルエンザにかかり、水泳をやめてしまいました」

　「アフリカに行ったことはないです。興味をそそられる大陸ですが、何にでくわすか予想もつきません」

　「鹿肉は珍味ですが、鹿を食べることに多少の抵抗感があります」

■対話に使える英文〔3〕
話し続けて！（でも冗長にならないように）

　「対話のキャッチボール」について、この章の冒頭でも触れましたが（p.163「双方向のコミュニケーション」）、もう少し詳しく話したいと思います。

　だれかに限定質問をされたとします。

　A: 休暇で外国に旅行するのが好きですか？
　B: はい。

　このような限定質問の後は、話を続けにくいものです。しかし、「質問と答え」ではなく対話になるよう、もう少し話し続けましょ

conversation, not just a Q&A. I always recommend that you keep talking for at least three sentences. If you respond with three sentences, you can give others the sense that you shared something about yourself. For example, you may want to say,

> B: Yes, I love going to different countries. My best vacation overseas was in Italy. I especially enjoyed the food and art in Florence.

Or you can say no:

> B: No, not really. I've been to Thailand, but the weather wasn't good while I was there. I guess I timed it wrong. I haven't tried another big trip since then.

Be sure to give the conversation ball to others after you speak for thirty seconds or so. When you receive an unexpected question, make sure to respond right away using one of the tactics mentioned in Chapter II, Keep speaking positively.

■ Try These in Your English Conversation [4]

Suspend judgment and ask questions

If you judge someone right away, it doesn't lead to a good conversation. However, not asking questions at all doesn't lead to a good conversation either. The point is, suspend judgment, and ask questions to get more information.

う。私はいつも、最低でも3文話し続けるようおすすめしています。3文かけて対応すると、相手はあなたに関する何かを教えてもらったと感じます。たとえば、以下のように話してみるのはいかがでしょうか。

　　B: はい、違う国に行くのが大好きです。一番楽しかった休暇はイタリアに行ったときでした。フローレンスの食べ物と芸術を満喫しました。

　または、否定的な答えでもかまいません。

　　B: いいえ、あんまり。タイに行ったことがありますが、滞在中、天候に恵まれませんでした。行った時期が悪かったんだと思います。それ以来、長い旅行には行っていません。

　30秒ぐらい続けて話したら、対話のボールを人に渡すように心がけます。また、意外な質問が来たときには、第2章の「積極的に話し続ける」（p.91）で述べた方法を使って、必ずすぐに何らかの応答をするようにします。

■対話に使える英文［4］
判断を保留して、質問する

　すぐさま相手を「こんな人だ」と判断してしまっては、よい対話に繋がりません。また、質問をしないと対話になりません。大事なのは、判断を保留しつつ質問をし、相手からもっと情報を引き出すことです。

Let's say someone told you about her new idea. You have doubts. But suspend judgment and ask probing questions.

"This is new to me. Have you done this before?"

"I see. It worked before. Can you share how that went?"

"Oh, it didn't work before. Can you share any insights or lessons learned from that?"

"Since it didn't work before, what are the differences that will help make it successful this time?"

"I see your point. Is there some data that also supports this idea?"

"This sounds like a good plan. How many people will we need to implement this?"

"It seems expensive. How much do you think it will cost?"

"I'm all for cost reduction. Where should we start?"

■ Try These in Your English Conversation [5]
How to say "No"

Japanese are famous for "not saying 'no.'" Most people around the world don't understand this, because making your position clear to others is one of the main purposes of communication. Also, saying "no" just shows that you don't agree on something. If you say "no" to others, they may be

仮に、ある女性が新しいアイデアを話してくれたとしましょう。あなたはそれがよいアイデアかどうか疑問に思っています。しかし、判断を保留して情報を探るための質問をします。

「これは聞いたことのないアイデアです。実行してみたことがありますか？」

「そうですか。前にうまくいったことがあるのですね。どんな感じだったか、話してもらえますか？」

「あぁ、うまくいかなかったんですね。そのご経験から得た洞察や学んだことを教えてもらえますか？」

「前はうまくいかなかったということなので、前回と違う点で、今回成功する要因となるものは何ですか？」

「おっしゃっていることはわかります。このアイデアの成功要因を示すデータがありますか？」

「なかなかいいプランですね。これを実施するのに必要な人員は？」

「費用がかさみそうですね。あなたの費用の見積もりは？」

「コスト削減には大賛成です。どこから始めましょうか？」

■対話に使える英文［5］
「ノー」と言うには

　日本人は「ノーと言わない」ということで有名です。自分の立場を明確にするのがコミュニケーションの主な目的ですから、海外の人は日本人のこの態度が理解できません。また、「ノー」と言うのは、あなたが何かに同意できないのを示すだけです。あなたが「ノー」と言えば、相手はがっかりするかもしれませんが、たいて

disappointed but they usually don't take it personally. They just understand that you don't like his/her opinion on something. Still, culturally, Japanese are hard-wired to think that we can harm our relationship with our conversation partners by saying "no." So, here are some examples for how to say "no" politely. The most important thing is that you include a reason when you say "no."

"Sorry, but Wednesday doesn't work for me. I have a prior engagement."

"I can't agree with you on this at this point. We still don't know which direction we are taking as a group."

"I'm not convinced that it'll work. How do you think our neighbors/colleagues/customers will react to this?"

"This timeline seems very optimistic. Do they really think we can make it? I don't want to take risks here."

"I'm not sure about this new design. It looks different, but the functions are the same."

"Unfortunately, we don't have the budget for this."

The following are some other options. Be sure to provide a reason following any of these phrases.

"That's a good argument/suggestion, but …"

"I see what you're saying, however …"

"That may not be correct because …"

いの場合、それを個人攻撃とは受け取りません。意見に賛同できない、と理解するだけです。しかし日本人は文化的に、「ノー」と言うと相手との人間関係を悪くしてしまうという考えを植え付けられています。ですから、ここに丁重に「ノー」と告げる例を挙げました。最も大切な点は、あなたの「ノー」の理由を必ず含めることです。

「すみません、水曜日は都合が悪いです。先約があります」

「現在の段階では、これには合意できません。グループ全体の進む方向がまだ決まってませんから」

「これがうまくいく確信が持てません。近所の人／同僚／顧客がこれにどう反応すると思いますか？」

「この実行計画は楽観的すぎるように思えます。彼らは本当にこの通りにいくと思っているんですか？ リスクを負担したくありません」

「この新しいデザインはどうかと思います。違うように見えますが、機能は前と同じですね」

「残念ながら、予算がありません」

　以下は、追加の例です。これらのフレーズの後に、必ず理由を加えてください。

「それはいい議論／提案ですが、……」

「おっしゃることはわかりますが、……」

「それは正しくないかもしれません、というのは……」

"I think the disadvantages of this idea are …"

"I understand where you're coming from, but …"

"I'm sorry, but I have to disagree with you on …"

[An excellent example]

One of my clients' colleagues is a Japanese gentleman who was not a skilled English speaker when he started working for an American company. He brought his lunch to the office every day. In his home-made lunch box or bento, he always packed three items: rice, fried eggs, and sausages. However, unlike most people who bring their lunch to work he never ate lunch at his desk. He always went to the company cafeteria, and had lunch with his colleagues. After several years, he has built a network of colleagues across the organization, earned their trust, and become a trusted manager. This is a prime example that you don't need beer or gourmet food to cultivate good relationships. You just need time and people to share good conversations with.

Final words on conversation in English

There are many differences between Japan and other countries. One of them always stands out to me.

Many people around the world learn Japanese because they want to communicate with Japanese. Japanese learn English, but we don't necessarily want to communicate with

「このアイデアの不都合な点は ……」

「あなたがそう考える理由はわかりますが、……」

「申し訳ありませんが、〜について反対せざるを得ません」

[素晴らしい事例]

　私のあるクライアントの同僚は日本人の男性で、アメリカ企業に勤め始めたころはたどたどしい英語を話していました。彼は、毎日お弁当を持ってきました。自分で詰めたお弁当には、いつもごはんと卵焼き、ソーセージが入っていました。しかし、お弁当持参組の他の人たちと違い、彼はけっして自分の机でランチを食べませんでした。彼は常に会社のカフェテリアへ行き、同僚とランチをともにしたのです。数年の間に、彼はその企業のいろんな部門で働く同僚たちとのネットワークを作り上げ、彼らの信用を得て、頼られる管理職になりました。これは、よい人間関係を築くのに、ビールも美食も要らないということの素晴らしい例です。あなたが必要なのは、対話をともにする時間と人なのです。

対話について、最後に一言

　日本と他の国との間には違う点がたくさんあります。その中で一つ、特に気になるものがあります。

　世界の多くの人が日本語を学ぶ理由は、日本人とコミュニケート（話したり、メールを交換したり）したいからです。日本人は英語を学びますが、必ずしも海外の人とコミュニケートしたいと

non-Japanese. This is a big difference and puzzling to most people who interact with Japanese. We want to learn things from foreigners too, but many of us prefer an indirect way: learning from English books.

This is kind of funny, because when we meet foreigners who speak a little bit of Japanese, we assume that they want to speak Japanese. However, the same can't be said about Japanese. Some Japanese who have a good command of English still don't want to speak in English. So, clearly, this is not just about our English skills.

I've heard the same questions/comments over and over in the U.S. The following two are what I hear most often:

"Do Japanese not like us?"
"He/she doesn't seem to care about us."

You may be shy. Or you may not want to make grammatical mistakes in front of others. But you certainly didn't mean to cause these types of misunderstandings. So, when you get a chance, please try to speak more often with people around the world. You don't have to speak English beautifully, but you need to show your interest in people and the topics of conversation. Besides, if you don't try to speak in English, how are you going to improve your English? Practice makes perfect. I hope you'll show your curiosity in people from different cultures, and enjoy learning about them.

思っているワケではありません。これは大きな違いで、日本人とやりとりする海外の人には理解しにくい点です。私たちも海外の人たちから学びたいとは思っているのですが、書籍を通じて間接的に学ぶのを好む人が多いのです。

　これはおかしなことです。というのは、私たちが日本語を多少話す海外の人に会うと、きっとその人は日本語を話したいのだろうと思います。しかし、同じことを日本人の英語学習について言うことはできません。日本人の中には、英語のスキルがあっても、英語を話したがらない人がいます。ですから明らかに、問題は英語力だけではないのです。

　アメリカで何度もくり返し受けた質問とコメントがあります。その中でも一番多く耳にしたのが、以下の二つです。

　　「日本人は私たちのことが嫌いなの？」
　　「あの人は私たちのことを、どうでもいいと思っているようだ」

　あなたは恥ずかしがり屋かもしれません。それとも、人前で文法的な間違いをおかしたくないと思っているかもしれません。しかし、このような誤解を招こうという意図はなかったはずです。ですから、チャンスがあれば、世界の人たちと進んで話してみてください。美しい英語を話す必要はありませんが、相手や話題に興味を示してください。それに、もし英語で話す努力をしなかったら、どうやって英語力を向上させるのでしょう？　習うより慣れよ、です。違う文化で育った人たちに好奇心を持って対応、彼らについての発見を楽しんでください。

❖ Summary ❖

Try to get to know each other through two-way and informal communication. Conversation is not a "presentation," so enjoying "playing catch" is the key to success.

Non-verbal communication like eye contact and posture is also an important component through which you can convey what you mean.

Expand your range of curiosity by exploring a new territory and acquiring new experiences.

Try not to be disappointed when you find differences from your conversation partners. Try to find something in common, and to discover something new about them by asking open-ended questions.

Avoid judging others quickly and spend time getting to know them.

Always explain reasons when you respond with "no."

Let's try the following:

· When you talk, keep eye contact for at least 5 seconds at a time.

· Begin your discussion with your point/conclusion, an interesting point or a problem to be solved in order to get your conversation partners interested in what you're going to say. If you tell your story in the sequence that the events occurred, you may lose your audience.

· Make a habit of having a clear conclusion to deliver before you start talking.

形式ばらない、双方向のコミュニケーションを通じて、お互いを知り合う努力をしよう。対話は「発表」ではないので、相手と話のキャッチボールを楽しむことが大切。

視線や姿勢などの非言語コミュニケーションも、あなたの意図を相手に正しく伝えるために大切な要素。

いろんな経験をして興味の幅を広げよう。

相手との違いにがっかりせず、共通点を見つけ、自由回答質問を使って相手をさらに知る努力を。

すぐに決めつけず、相手の考え方を知る努力を。

「ノー」で返事をするときは、必ず理由を添えよう。

やってみよう

・相手の目を見て話し、目を合わせたら最低でも5秒間は視線をそらさない。

・時系列を追って話すのではなく、結論や面白い点または解決すべき問題について話し始め、相手の興味をつなぎとめよう。

・話し始める前に、結論を明確にしておく習慣をつけよう。

Chapter V

Global English

By stepping outside of your native country, you'll come to know even more about your own culture. Of course, you know your country's history, way of living, landscapes, and such. But we rarely think deeply about our cultural values, beliefs, and assumptions. Living and working overseas will give you another level of appreciation of what Japanese culture is.

Our ways of thinking and doing are part of our culture. Of course, each individual has his or her ways, but as a people of a nation, we tend to have a strong tendency to think and do things in certain ways. In Japan, we bow when we meet, take our shoes off when we go into the house. We tend to have many meetings before we decide on something as a group. We tend to have a strong need to take care of the details first so that our plans will be executed smoothly. And these tendencies are not universal around the world. So, our common sense is

第5章

グローバルな英語

　自分の生まれ育った国から一歩出ると、自分の文化がより鮮明にわかります。もちろん、自分の国の歴史や暮らし方、風景などは知っています。けれども、自国にいながら自分の文化の価値観や信念、当たり前と考えられていることについて、深く吟味することはまれです。海外で暮らしたり、働いたりすることで、日本文化をより深く理解するようになります。

　考え方や、やり方は、文化の一部です。もちろん、人それぞれのやり方もありますが、国全体で見ると、私たちはある一定の考え方ややり方に従う傾向の強い国民です。日本では、誰かに会うときは頭を下げますし、家に上がるときは靴を脱ぎます。グループで何かを決める前に、会議を何度もくり返します。何かに取り組むときは、計画が問題なく実行されるよう、詳細にまつわる問題をまず解明する必要性を強く感じがちです。このような傾向は、世界共通のものではありません。ですから、私たちの常識は、世界の常識ではありません。

not a global common sense.

Culture also influences our English. Our English has a Japanese cultural flavor. And this can create obstacles in our communication in English. How can we speak and write in English in a way that everyone in the world can understand easily?

Reduce Japanese cultural influence on your English

■ Japanese Cultural Influences [1]
Cases of "lost in translation"

I can think of four "lost in translation" cases that we tend to commit in English conversation. They happen because we attach a certain meaning to a Japanese word, and assume that its meaning is universal.

ⓐ Difficult

When we say to someone, "This may be difficult," it is to convey the message, "It's impossible," or "I'm sorry, but we can't do it." But most Westerners think, "It is difficult, and thus it's worth doing. If it's easy, everyone will do it." "Being difficult" in English means "it's a challenge" and Westerners can get pumped up for a challenge. Meanwhile, Japanese may scratch their heads and say, "We told them we can't do it. Why do they keep coming back with the same thing?"

日本文化は、私たちの英語にも影響します。私たちの英語には、日本文化の味付けがされているのです。そしてこれが英語のコミュニケーションの障害となることがあります。世界の誰もがわかってくれる英語を話したり書いたりするには、どうすればよいのでしょうか？

日本文化の影響を減らす

■日本文化の影響［1］

翻訳のズレが誤解を招く

　英語で対話するときにやってしまいがちな「翻訳のズレ」の例を四つ紹介します。ズレの原因は、私たちが日本語の単語に当てはめた特定の意味を、世界共通と思い込んでしまうことです。

ⓐ Difficult

　日本人が誰かに「難しいかもね」と言うとき、それは「不可能だな」とか、「すみませんが、できません」という意味を伝えようとしてのことです。しかし欧米人のほとんどは、「難しい、だからこそやる価値がある。簡単だったら、だれでもするよ」と考えます。英語で「難しい」は、「チャレンジだ」という意味で、挑戦に向けてやる気満々になります。そこで日本人は、頭をかきながら「できないって言ったのになぁ。どうして同じ案件の話をぶり返すんだろう？」と言うのです。

When I started to express myself in English, I sometimes felt that Americans didn't care about what I was saying. It took a long time for me to recognize a pattern. I was using Japanese *tokorode* before I tried to steer the conversation in a direction that I wanted to go. And for the word *tokorode* I used "by the way." Unfortunately, "by the way" can mean "this is an additional point (therefore it's not the main point)" or "this is an afterthought." No wonder they didn't care what I said after "by the way." I should've said my main point only.

"Well, I'm also interested in the package design."

"I want us to think about what kind of training program will be needed before we launch the new product in the market."

"My main point is that we need to make sure that every customer can expect the same level of customer service from our dealers.

ⓒ Study

How do you interpret the phrase "I'll study your report"? Americans' responses to this question vary from "Well, they're not interested," or "It's just a stalling tactic," to "Well, my Japanese boss actually reads my report, so it's positive." Many non-Japanese agonize over the word "study." It's mainly

　英語で話し始めたばかりのとき、私の発言にアメリカ人はおかまいなしだという印象を、ときどき受けました。あるパターンに気づくのに、けっこう時間がかかりました。話したい方向へ対話を誘導したいとき、私は日本語の「ところで」を使っていました。そして、日本語の「ところで」の訳に "by the way" を使っていました。残念ながら、"by the way" は、「これは追加のポイントですが（重要なポイントではありません）」もしくは、「あとで思いついたことですが」という意味なのです。どうりで私が "by the way" の後に述べた内容を気にかけてくれなかったワケです。私は "by the way" を省いて、　以下のように伝えたいポイントだけ言うべきでした。

　　「パッケージのデザインにも興味があります」

　　「新製品を市場に出す前に、どんな研修プログラムが必要かを
　　　考えるべきです」

　　「大事なポイントは、どの顧客もディーラーから同じレベルの
　　　顧客サービスを期待できるようにしなければならないという
　　　ことです」

ⓒ **Study**

　日本人の「あなたの報告書を検討（study）します」を、どのように解釈しますか？　この質問に対するアメリカ人の返答は、「興味がない」「対応を遅らせるための手」から、「私の日本人のボスは私の報告書をちゃんと読みます。だから肯定的な対応」までさまざまです。海外の人の多くは日本人の「検討」に悩まされます。主

because this word is usually not used in business. People study something for their own learning, so Westerners can't be sure what Japanese mean by "study."

Also, Japanese tend to say "We need to study" as their final statement, and don't say much about what will happen after they have studied it. Moreover, Japanese don't say anything about the report that they've just received, even though their counterparts are sitting right in front of them. The following are good examples that have additional information, comments or questions.

"I need to study this. Please give me a couple of days, as it takes time for me to read English. I'll get back to you by Wednesday."

"Thank you for the report. The answers to my questions may be in this report. But can I ask you a couple of questions?"

"Thank you. This report helps us confirm the progress we've made so far. What are the major differences between this quarter and the last?"

❹ Had better

I don't hear this phrase very much anymore, but want to you know that in the U.S., the use of the phrase "had better" can cause a serious misunderstanding. If you use this phrase when you suggest that others do something, they may think that you're threatening them. In a sensitive situation, they

な理由は study という単語が通常ビジネスで使われない単語だからです。Study は自分の学習のためにすることなので、欧米人にはピンとこないのです。

また、日本人は「検討が必要です」を最後の発言として言うことが多く、その後の展開についてあまり述べません。さらに、報告書をくれた人が目の前に座っているのに、報告書について何も言わない人もいます。以下は、展開を加えたよい例です。

「ゆっくり読ませてください。英語を読むのに時間がかかるので、２日ほどかかります。水曜日までに連絡します」

「報告書、ありがとうございます。私の質問に対する答えはこの報告書に入っているかもしれませんが、二つほど質問してもいいですか？」

「ありがとうございます。この報告書で、いままでの進捗を確認できます。この四半期と前の四半期との大きな違いは何ですか？」

🔴 Had better

最近この間違いをあまり耳にしなくなりましたが、アメリカでは大きな誤解のもとになる表現です。あなたがこの表現を使って何か行動を勧めると、相手はあなたに威嚇されたと思うので、使わないようにしましょう。状況がややこしい場合は、セクハラやパワハラと受け取られかねません。ですから、相手に行動を示唆

may even think that your comments were sexual harassment or power harassment. So, please avoid using this phrase when you recommend an action to others. Although you may find a Japanese translation in a dictionary that describes this phrase is a "gentle suggestion," this is not the case in the U.S. Instead, use the following expressions.

> You may want to …
> I'd like you to …
> I recommend that …

However, you can use this phrase when you're talking about yourself.

> "I'd better leave now, otherwise I'll miss my train."
>
> "I'd better finish this work so that I can go to the concert tomorrow."
>
> "I'd better buy a present this weekend, otherwise I'll be going to the party empty-handed."

■ Japanese Cultural Influences [2]
Think about "think"

When we speak and write in Japanese, we tend to add "think" at the end of sentences. This is often because we want to be polite when we express our views and opinions, and also to avoid coming across as pushy or judgmental. So, quite naturally,

する場合は、この表現を使わないようにしましょう。英和辞書にはこの表現を「親切な提案」のように記述してありますが、アメリカ英語には当てはまりません。提案をする場合は、以下のような表現を使ってください。

> You may want to …
> I'd like you to …
> I recommend that …

ただし、自分のことに関しては使えます。

> 「今出ないと、電車に乗り遅れる」
> 「明日のコンサートに行けるように、今日この仕事を終わらせなければいけない」
> 「今週末にプレゼントを買わないと、パーティーに手ぶらで行くハメになる」

■日本文化の影響［2］
"think" について考える

私たちが日本語で話したり書いたりするとき、文の最後を「と思います」で締めくくることが多いです。これは多くの場合、自分の見方や意見を話すとき礼儀正しくありたいということと、押しが強いとか決めつけているなどと思われたくないからです。で

we often start our English sentences with "I think" or "We think." However, saying "I think" too many times can make you look less confident. The Western world is built on the idea, "I think, therefore I am," so Westerners assume that everyone has thought about the topic before he/she speaks out. So, "I think" is sometimes unnecessary, and can even dilute your message.

For example, if someone asks you, "Can you finish this by Wednesday?" how would you respond? If you are confident, you should say, "Sure, I can," or "Things are going as expected, so I'm confident that we can get it done by Wednesday," or something like that. These statements sound much more confident than "I think I can" or "I think we can." I learned this through my own experience. When I answered, "I think I can," my counterpart asked me back, "You think you can?" with a doubtful eye.

■ Japanese Cultural Influences [3]
Alternatives to "think"

However, eliminating "think" from your sentences may make your English blunt. So, we need alternatives to the word "think." The good news is that there are many to choose from. Here are some of the most common options:

- **Imagine**   I never imagined that I would have a cat.
- **Believe**   I believe that this cat will be a good companion to you.

すから自然に、英文を "I think" や "We think" で始めます。しかし、"I think" を言いすぎると、自信がなさそうに聞こえてしまいます。欧米の社会は「我思う、故に我あり」という考えの上に成り立っていますから、その人なりに話題に関する考えがあるのは当然とみなします。ですから、"I think" が不要のときもありますし、"I think" のせいで説得力が薄れてしまうことさえあります。

　たとえば、「水曜日までにこれを完了できますか？」と聞かれたとしましょう。もし水曜日までに終える自信があれば、「もちろん」や「状況が予定通りにうまくいっているので、水曜日までに完了する自信があります」などと言うのがいいでしょう。このような返答のほうが、「できると思います」より、話し手の自信を伝えられます。これは、私の経験からも言えることです。私が「できると思います」と返事をしたら、相手が「できると思う？」と疑わしそうに私を見たのです。

Think以外の選択肢

　しかし、"think" を完全に取り除いてしまうと、ぶっきらぼうな英語になってしまいます。ですから、"think" に代わる選択肢が必要です。好都合なことに、多くの選択肢があります。以下にあげるのは、よく使われる単語です。

- 猫を飼うことになるとは想像もつきませんでした。

- この猫はなかなかよい相棒になると思います。

- **Trust**   I trust that this cat won't scratch people.

- **Hope**   I hope that this cat will behave herself.

- **Expect**   I expect this cat to learn how to behavior.

- **Agree**   I agree that some cats are teachable.

- **Consider** If not, I'll consider having the cat declawed.

- **I'm afraid** I'm afraid that we need to have the cat declawed.

- **Suppose** I suppose that teaching cats is impossible.

- **Disagree** I respectfully disagree. You may want to give your cat a chance.

By using these verb choices instead of "think" you can convey what you want to say more clearly with a hint of feelings and attitude. Some Japanese seem to think that we need to use ice-cold logic when we speak English, but I don't find this to be true. We certainly want to be clear about yes or no, for example, but people all over the world speak their languages to get connected and understand each other. English isn't an exception to this. So, by adding these alternatives to your vocabulary, you can express yourself more clearly and with a touch of feeling, and you also increase your chances of building good relationships with people around the world.

■ Japanese Cultural Influences [4]

Be-verbs vs. Action-verbs

There are two kinds of verbs: Linking verbs like "to be" and

- この猫は人をひっかかないと確信しています。

- この猫がおりこうにしてくれますように。

- この猫はおりこうになるでしょう。

- 確かに、新しいことを学べる猫もいますね。

- 学ばなければ、猫の爪をとってもらいます。

- 猫の爪をとる手術が必要になると思います。

- おそらく猫に教えるのは不可能です。

- 失礼ながら、反対します。あなたの猫にチャンスをあげてください。

　Think のかわりにこれらの動詞を使うことで、あなたの気持ちや態度をほのめかしつつ、言いたいことをより明確に伝えられます。英語で話すときは、理論一辺倒でなければいけないと考える日本人もいますが、私はそうは思いません。もちろん、yes か no かなどははっきりしなければいけませんが、世界中の人たちが言語を使ってお互いを知り、理解するのです。英語も例外ではありません。ですから、これらの動詞をあなたの語彙に加えることで、より明確に気持ちを込めて自分を表現でき、そして世界中の人とのよい人間関係を、もっと築けるようになります。

■日本文化の影響［4］
be動詞 vs. アクション動詞

　動詞には2種類あります。be動詞のように言葉と言葉をつなぐ

Action-verbs. "To be" is the main Linking verb, with are/am/ is/are and their past and past participle forms. I call them Be-verbs for short. When I first learned English a long time ago, we started with "This is a pen." However, in the last twenty-six years of living in the U.S., I have never had a chance to say or write that sentence. In adult communication, we usually don't state the obvious.

Be-verbs and Action-verbs can explain one of the differences between native English and Japanese English. Japanese language is full of Be-verbs. I'm a teacher. I'm an engineer. I'm a homemaker. Therefore, we tend to feel more comfortable when we start a sentence with "a subject + Be-verb." But when we speak with Be-verbs, our messages tend to become vague and weak. Please compare the following sentences.

Be-verb: I'm a teacher.

Action-verb: I teach Social Studies in high school.

Be-verb: I'm an engineer at ABC company.

Action-verb: I'm working on a new chip design at ABC company.

Be-verb: I'm a stay-at-home mom (or dad).

Action-verb: I manage my family's finance and schedules and health.

You might say that you want to say both. "I'm a teacher,

動詞と、アクション動詞です。are/am/is/are と、その過去形と過去分詞形などが主な「つなぎ動詞」で、be動詞と呼びます。ずっと前に初めて英語を学んだとき、"This is a pen." という文を最初に習いました。しかし、二十数年アメリカで暮らす中で、この文を言ったり書いたりする機会にはまだ巡り合っていません。大人のコミュニケーションでは、通常、わかり切っていることを述べません。

be動詞とアクション動詞で、ネィティブの英語と日本語英語の違いの一つを説明できます。日本語にはbe動詞があふれています。「私は先生です」「私はエンジニアです」「私は主婦（主夫）です」。私たちは「主語 + be動詞」で文を始めるのに慣れています。しかし、be動詞で話すとメッセージがぼんやりし、弱くなります。以下の文を比較してください。

（am）　　　：私は教師です。

（teach）　：私は高校で社会を教えています。

（am）　　　：私はABC会社のエンジニアです。

（work）　：私はABC会社で新しいチップのデザインをしています。

（am）　　　：私は家事に専念する母親（父親）です。

（manage）：私は我が家の家計と、日程、健康を管理しています。

be動詞とアクション動詞の両方を使いたいと思われる方もい

and teach Social Studies in high school." This is not wrong. However, in business conversation, less is more. Some native speakers may feel that English spoken by Japanese is verbose (too many words) or convoluted (complicated). Please see the next example.

"I think" + Be-verb: I think it is necessary for us to tackle this item before it becomes a problem.
(16 words)

Be-verb: It is necessary for us to tackle this item before it becomes a problem. (14 words)

Action-verb: We need to tackle this item before it becomes a problem. (11 words)

By eliminating "I think" and "it is" you can communicate your point faster and more clearly.

■ Japanese Cultural Influences [5]
The first three words

In Japan, we are taught that we listen to others until they finish their story. However, if we speak English in our natural Japanese way, chances are others will cut in and can take the conversation in other directions or even start talking about a new subject. As a result, we can lose the opportunity to complete our thoughts and communicate the main point of our story. On the East Coast of the U.S., in reality we won't be able

るでしょう。「私は先生で、高校で社会を教えています」。これは間違いではありませんが、ビジネスの対話では、すっきりとまとめる方が効果的です。ネイティブ・スピーカーの中には、日本人の英語は冗長だとか、要素が絡み合いすぎて主要な筋が読み取れない、と感じる人もいます。以下をご覧ください。

"I think"+ is : I think it is necessary for us to tackle this item before it becomes a problem.
（単語数16）

(is)　　　　 : It is necessary for us to tackle this item before it becomes a problem. （単語数14）

(need)　　　 : We need to tackle this item before it becomes a problem. （単語数11）

　"I think"と"it is"を省くことで、言いたいことをより早く、そしてより明確に伝えることができます。

■日本文化の影響［5］
最初の3単語

　日本では、人の話を最後まで聞くようにと言われて育ちます。けれども、日本人に自然なやり方で英語を話すと、人が横入りして対話を別の方向へ持っていくか、もしくは、全く新しい話題に切り替えてしまうかです。その結果、考えていたことを言いきって、話の重要なポイントを伝える機会を逃してしまいます。アメリカの東海岸では、実際のところ、文を言い終えることすらできません。これは、ペースの速い東海岸の地域文化の影響でもあり

to finish our sentences. This is in part a reflection of the fast-paced regional culture, but also due to how English sentences are structured. As we all know, most English sentences start with a subject and a verb. As soon as they hear the first verb, they think they understood your position.

I agree with you, …
I'm not convinced, as …
I still hope that …

So, we need to state our main points right up front and emphasize the verb by saying that word a bit louder and possibly with a slightly higher tone. In English, stress, not intonation, is primarily used to emphasize the key point of the sentence. When you stress a word, you pronounce it strongly and punctuate it with a little push. Intonation (speaking in a slightly higher tone of voice) can also help, however, stressing the verb and pronouncing it clearly is more effective. Stress is not used in Japanese language, so this can be a challenge.

However, we can at least avoid using Japanese rhythm and tone of voice in English sentences. I'll show you some examples.

"I had a meeting with Mr. Tanaka yesterday."

When speaking in a natural Japanese rhythm, some Japanese will tend to raise their tone (not using stress) at

ますが、英語の文の構成にも起因しています。ご存じのように、英語の文のほとんどは主語と動詞で始まります。最初の動詞を聞いた瞬間に、聞き手はあなたの観点がわかったと思うのです。

賛成です。

確信が持てません。

まだ希望を持っています。

ですから、私たちは自分たちが一番言いたいことをまず最初に言い、また動詞を少し大きめに、少し高めの音で話す必要があります。英語では、抑揚（声の高さを少し上げて話す）ではなく、強勢を使って文の重要点を強調します。強勢をつけて話すには、その単語を強く発音し、また前に押す感じで強調します。抑揚も助けにはなりますが、強勢を使って動詞をはっきり発音することのほうが効果的です。強勢は日本語を話すときには使いせんので、日本人は難しいと感じるかもしれません。

けれども少なくとも、日本語のリズムと音調で英語を話すことを避けるよう心がけてください。以下の例をご覧ください。

"I had a meeting with Mr. Tanaka yesterday."

日本語の自然なリズムで話すとき、yesterday で（強勢を使わずに）音の高さを上げがちです。会議が昨日だったことを強調した

"yesterday." This may not have been their point, unless they wanted to emphasize the fact that the meeting took place yesterday.

A: Did you talk about this with Mr. Tanaka last week?
B: No, I discussed this with him yesterday. So, I didn't get the update until then.

In the above dialogue, it is natural to stress "yesterday," as you want to communicate the fact that you saw Mr. Tanaka yesterday with the newly acquired information.

So, try to use stress more than the tone of your voice in order to make your point clear. Also, be sure to stress the verb or the word that you want to emphasize.

■Japanese Cultural Influences [6]
Be ready for questions that we don't usually ask each other

Common sense develops within a culture. So, please be aware that our Japanese common sense may not be common among people outside of Japan. We're all born into a culture and don't challenge customs that are considered to be right. If you do, you'll probably be scolded, and will eventually learn how to behave within the culture. We want to belong to the culture and be comfortable with it and also want our friends and neighbors to be comfortable around us.

For the same reason, people outside of Japan have their

場合を除いて、おそらく「昨日」はこの文の主要な点ではありません。

    A: これについて、田中さんと先週話しましたか？
    B: いいえ、彼と話し合えたのは<u>昨日</u>でした。ですから、それまで最新情報を得られませんでした。

　上記の会話では、田中さんに会って新しい情報を得たのは昨日だったということを伝えたいので、「昨日」に強勢を置くのが自然です。

　自分の言いたいことを相手に明確に伝えられるよう、抑揚より強勢を使うようにしてください。また、動詞やあなたが強調したい単語に強勢を置くようにしてください。

■ 日本文化の影響 [6]
日本人どうしでは尋ねない質問への心がまえ

　常識はそれぞれの文化の中で作られます。ですから、日本の常識が海外では通用しないかもしれないことを、常に胸に留めておいてください。人間はみな特定の文化の中で生まれ、そこで正しいとされる習慣の正当性を疑いません。もし抵抗すると、怒られ、その文化の中でどう振舞うかを、いずれは身につけます。生まれ育った文化に属し、その中で居心地よく暮らしたいですし、また、友だちや近所の人たちに、不愉快な思いをさせたくないとも思います。

　これと同じ理由で、海外の人たちにも自分の文化圏の人たちと

own common sense that they share with people of their own culture. And Japanese common sense may be foreign to them. Let's say that in your friend's culture it is common sense to keep their shoes on inside the house. How would you answer the question, "Why do you need to take your shoes off when you go into someone's house in Japan?"

For people who didn't grow up in Japan, some things don't make sense. In their effort to figure things out, they may ask you questions that you may have never considered in your life. When you go outside of Japan you may need to learn other cultures—as the famous proverb goes, "When in Rome, do as the Romans do." However, when you're in Japan, or even outside of Japan, you may come across these cultural questions that you need to answer. Be ready to explain things to the Romans and people from other cultures.

One of the funniest questions that I've ever encountered was "Can I put my sashimi in a hot pot? I can't eat raw fish, but they look so good!" If you were in my shoes, how would you answer?

■ Japanese Cultural Influences [7]

Be aware that the Japanese belief system is unique

World religions like Christianity, Judaism, and Islam have one god. Historically most people in ancient times believed in multiple gods that existed in nature and their imagination. But

共有する常識があります。そして、日本の常識が彼らにとっては意外に感じられるかもしれません。たとえば、あなたの友だちの文化では、家の中でも靴を履くのが常識だとしましょう。「日本でよその家に上がるときは、どうして靴を脱がなければならないの？」と聞かれたらどう答えますか？

　日本で育たなかった人には、理屈に合わないことがあります。海外の人は日本の物事を理解しようとして、あなたが今まで考えたこともない質問をしてくるかもしれません。有名な「郷に入っては郷に従え」の諺にもあるように、海外に出ていくと他国の文化を学ばなければなりません。しかし、日本にいる場合、また場合によっては海外にいても、日本文化に関する質問に出くわし、答えなければならないことがあります。文化を異にする人たちに日本文化を説明する準備をしておきましょう。

　今までに私が受けた質問の中で一番おかしかったのは、「刺身を鍋に入れてもいいですか？　私は刺身が食べられませんが、とてもおいしそうです」というものです。あなたが私の立場だったら、どう答えますか？

■日本文化の影響 [7]
日本の信仰形態は独特

　キリスト教やユダヤ、イスラム教などの世界の宗教は、一神教です。歴史的には、ほとんどの古代人が、自然や想像の世界に存在した多くの神を信じていました。しかし、しだいにほとんどの

then many of them moved on to believing in one omnipotent (all-mighty) god who created the universe or manages it or both.

As it is any people's tendency, those who believe in one god tend to see those who believe a different god or believe in more than one god as primitive or less-developed. And most Japanese fall under this category, as we believe or practice Shinto by going to Shinto shrines. Also, according to Kojiki or Records of Ancient Matters, we have eight million gods.

And another aspect can add more to the mystery for non-Japanese. Outside of Japan very few people combine two different religions together into their belief system. In Japan though, we don't see a conflict or contradiction in believing and practicing Shinto and Buddhism together. This is the long-lasting impact of the syncretic fusion of Shintoism and Buddhism (*Shinbutsu Shugou*) that was initiated in the Nara period. According to the CIA's *World Factbook*, the percentages of the religions practiced in Japan (Shintoism 70.4%, Buddhism 69.8%, Christianity 1.5%, other 6.9%) confirm this fusion of religions because the total percentage is greater than the population in Japan.*

And the mystery doesn't even end here. What is your answer to the question, "What is your religion?" Most Japanese

---

*The CIA's analysis is consistent with Japanese government statistics, which are available on a portal called "Statistics of Japan."

人が、宇宙を創造したか管理しているか、もしくはその両方を担う全能の神を信じるようになりました。

　これは人類に共通の傾向ですが、ある神を信じる人は別の神を信じる人や多神教を信じる人を原始的だとか、知的に未発達の人だと考えます。日本人のほとんどは、日本独特の宗教である神道を信じているか、神社にお参りに行くなど神道を実践しているので、この中に入ります。古事記によれば、日本列島には八百万の神が住んでいるとも言われています。

　海外の人にとって、もう一つ不思議なことがあります。日本以外では、二つの宗教を一つの信仰形態に統合した例は非常に少ないのです。しかし日本では、神道と仏教をともに信仰しそれぞれの宗教行為を行うことに対立や矛盾を感じません。これは、奈良時代に始まった神仏習合の歴史的な影響です。CIA刊の『ザ・ワールド・ファクトブック』によると、日本の信仰は、神道が70.4%、仏教が69.8%、キリスト教が1.5%、その他の宗教が6.9%となっていて、宗教を信仰する人の総計が人口を上回っており、複数の宗教信仰が行われていることを示しています*。

　不思議な点はそれだけではありません。「あなたの信仰は何ですか?」と聞かれたら、何と答えますか? ほとんどの日本人は、

---

* 2018年の日本政府の統計データについては「e-Stat統計で見る日本」を参照のこと

respond, "I don't have a religion." We tend to hesitate to say, "I believe in X," because many of us don't pray regularly, visit a place of worship regularly, and haven't really learned about our own religion. However, most of us visit Shinto shrines at the end of the year or at the beginning of a new year. Some celebrate the birth of a child, and children's coming of age of three, five, seven, and twenty years old there. Some get married at a Shinto shrine. And yet, when we die, most of us have a grave stone at a Buddhist temple. And some of us, like myself, get married under Christianity. This is beyond most people's imagination in the world.

So, what is the best way to answer the question, "What is your religion?" I usually say that I believe in Shinto, as I always go back to a Shinto shrine in my hometown when I visit my father. Shinto is an animistic religion that worships natural elements like old trees and rivers, lakes and rocks, as well as our ancestors and local gods. Shinto in that sense is very similar to the Native American belief system. That's how I explain my belief. Please take some time and think about your own response to this question.

If you're uncomfortable saying, "I believe …" you may want to say, "I practice Shinto (or any religion you practice)." Most of us may not know or believe in the theology of a religion, but we certainly practice a religion or two by going to a Shinto shrine and/or a Buddhist temple or any other place of worship.

「宗教はありません」と答えます。多くの日本人は定期的に祈ったり、信仰の場に通ったり、自分の宗教について学んだりしませんから、「私はこれこれの宗教を信じています」と言うのをためらいます。しかし、大晦日かお正月にはほとんどの人が神社に参拝します。子どもの誕生や七五三、成人式を神社でお祝いする人もいます。神式で結婚する人もいます。しかし、この世を去ると、私たちのほとんどはお寺にあるお墓に入ります。中には私のように、教会で結婚式を挙げる人もいます。これは世界の人たちの多くにとって、想像すらできないことなのです。

　では、「あなたの宗教は何ですか？」という質問に、どう答えればいいのでしょうか？　私は普段、神道を信じていると答えます。なぜなら、日本へ帰省し父に会うたびに、地元の神社へ行くからです。神道は祖先や地域の神々だけでなく、自然の中に存在するもの、たとえば大樹や、川、湖、岩などを崇拝する自然崇拝の宗教です。その意味で、神道はアメリカ・インディアンの信仰に似ています。私はこんな風に自分の信仰を説明します。この質問に対するあなたの返答を、じっくり考えてみてください。

　もし、「信仰する」というのに違和感がある場合は、「神道（またはあなたが実践している宗教）を実践しています」というのはいかがでしょうか。ほとんどの日本人は、それぞれの宗教の神学的なことを知らなかったり、信じていなかったりしますが、実際には神社に参拝したり、お寺に行ったり（もしくはその両方）、または他の宗教の場で祈ったりするので、一つか二つの宗教を実践していると言えるのです。

Avoid becoming defensive

Every culture has a few taboo questions that its people avoid asking. In the U.S., those are political and religion-related questions, as they tend to trigger strong emotions and it can be difficult to have a calm and meaningful conversation about them. For Japanese, one of the taboo questions concerns the wars, especially the Second World War.

Americans and Japanese reasons for avoiding touchy subjects are slightly different. Most Americans have their opinions and are aware that their opinions may conflict with others' opinions. On the other hand, many Japanese are not sure how they feel or what they think about the wars, as we haven't spent time thinking about them.

One of the touchy subjects for Americans is gun control. In the U.S., political affiliation and religious affiliation in many cases go together. Therefore, a policy-related or political question can be seen as an attack on their belief system. And, people can get emotional about it.

When you're emotional about something, you tend to become easily offended and criticize others harshly, or become overly defensive. For most Japanese and other Asians, becoming defensive when you're communicating in English can be problematic, as it can negatively impact people's

批評に対して神経をとがらせない

　どの文化にも、避けるべきタブーの質問があります。アメリカ
では、政治と宗教に関連する質問がそれです。非常に感情的な反
応を引き起こすので、政治と宗教について、冷静で深い会話をす
るのはアメリカでは難しいのです。日本人にとってのタブーな質
問は、戦争、特に第二次世界大戦に関するものです。

　アメリカ人と日本人が扱いにくい話題を避ける理由は、多少異
なります。ほとんどのアメリカ人は自分なりの意見を持ってい
て、自分の意見が相手の意見と衝突するかもしれないことを知っ
ています。いっぽう、日本人には、戦争に関して自分が何を感じ
ているのか、考えているのかを自覚していない人が多いのです。
これは私たちが、この話題について時間をかけて考えたことがな
いからです。

　アメリカ人が神経をとがらせる話題の一つに銃規制がありま
す。アメリカでは、支持する政党と信仰する宗教との間に強い関
連性があります。ですから、政策関連または政治関連の質問は、
宗教への攻撃と見られがちです。それで、感情的になってしまう
のです。

　人は誰しも、何かについて感情的になるとムッとして人をひど
く批判したり、過度の自己防衛に走ったりします。日本人と他の
アジア人が英語で話しているときに、批評や非難に対して神経過
敏になってしまうと、状況を悪くしてしまいます。あなたの人と
しての評判を下げてしまうからです。例を使って、「防衛的」な態

perception of you as a person. Let me explain "defensive" attitudes through an example.

At a workshop that I led at a Japanese company in the U.S., two Americans started talking about a gun control during a break. This is a very sensitive subject. One of them was a strong proponent of people's right to bear arms, as per the Second Amendment of the U.S. Constitution. The other one avoided giving a clear-cut answer to this issue. He had lived in countries where guns were outlawed and liked living a life with no worries about guns. Right away, the differences of their opinions were clear. The defender of the constitutional right raised his voice and said definitively, "Guns can't commit crimes. We should blame people who don't know how to use guns!" And the other one said, "I know, but if you have guns and you're afraid of something or somebody, you may pull the trigger and end up killing innocent people." Then, he asked me "What do you think, Michiko?" Oh, please don't get me involved in this! But I had to say something. Honesty is my best strategy, so I responded, "Well, I grew up in Japan where civilians can't carry guns, and gun-related crimes existed only in movies. I felt very safe there as I grew up." With that, the gun advocate stormed out of the training room.

New York and New Jersey, where the workshop took place, have much stricter gun controls than many other states. So, this person who lived in the state where many people carry guns may have felt uneasy coming to New Jersey. He may

度についてもう少し説明します。

　アメリカのある日系企業でワークショップをしたときのこと
です。休憩時間に、二人のアメリカ人が銃規制について話し始め
ました。これは非常に慎重さを要する話題です。そのうちの一人
は、アメリカの憲法の修正条項第2条で保証されている「国民が
銃砲を所有し携帯する権利」の強い支持者でした。もう一人は、こ
の案件について明確な返答を避けました。彼は銃の保持が違法と
される国々に住んだことがあり、銃について心配せずに暮らせた
ことを好ましく思っていました。二人の意見の違いは一目瞭然で
した。憲法で保障された権利の弁護者は、声を荒らげ、「銃は犯罪
を犯せない。銃の使い方を知らない人を責めるべきだ」ときっぱ
り言い切りました。これに対しもう一人は、「わかってるよ。で
も銃を持っているときに、誰かや何かに恐怖心を抱いたら引き金
を引いてしまい、罪のない人を間違って殺してしまうかもしれな
い」と言いました。そして、彼は私に「ミチコ、どう思う？」と聞
いてきたのです。お願いだから、私を巻きぞえにしないでよ！　と
思いましたが、黙っているわけにはいきません。正直であること
が最善の方策と思っているので、「そうですね、私が育った日本
は一般市民は銃を持てない社会で、銃の絡んだ犯罪は映画の中だ
けの存在でした。銃犯罪について心配することなく育ちました」
と答えました。すると、銃保持権利の提唱者は研修室を飛び出て
行ってしまったのです。

　ニューヨーク州とワークショップが行われたニュージャー
ジー州には、他州に比べずっと厳しい銃規制があります。ですか
ら、多くの人が銃を携帯する州に住むこの人は、ニュージャー
ジー州に来て、その違いに居心地の悪さを感じたのかもしれませ

also have felt that his view was challenged, threatened, and even criticized by the other person and me, even though that wasn't our intention. The other person and I only explained our position and its reasoning.

Everyone is entitled to have their own views. And everyone can and needs to defend their own views when necessary. However, if you become defensive, then your words and attitudes often project a negative and weak image of yourself. If you feel challenged, threatened, or criticized, please try using the suggestions below. You can apply these to difficult conversations on any subject.

◆ Path to Mastery 13

1. Take a deep breath

2. Focus on explaining your views

3. Stay civil and enjoy exchanging different views

4. Withhold your judgment and avoid dichotomy. In order to show that you're not judging and attacking the other side, please avoid the following sets of words:

o "right" and "wrong"
o "good" and "bad"
o "always" and "never"

5. Stay calm—don't raise your voice or get physical

ん。また、彼は自分の見方が問いただされ、追い詰められ、非難されているとさえ感じたのかもしれません。私たちにはそのような意図はなく、自分の意見と理由を説明しただけだったのですが。

　誰もが自分の意見を持つ権利があります。そして、必要であれば自分の見方を弁護することができますし、するべきです。しかし自分の意見を過剰防衛すると、あなたの言葉や態度から、悪い印象や、あなたが弱い人だという印象を与えてしまいます。もし、問いただされ、追い詰められ、非難されていると感じたら、以下のことを試してみてください。これは、難しい対話をするときにも使えます。

◆ コミュニケーションの極意 13

1. 深呼吸する

2. あなたの意見を説明することに集中する (相手を負かそうとしない)

3. マナーを守り、違う意見の交換を楽しむ

4. 相手を独善的に判断してしまったり、意見を真っ二つに分けないようにする。あなたが相手を独善的に判断したり攻撃していないことを示すために、以下の3組の言葉を使わないようにしてください。
   - ○ 「正しい」と「間違い」
   - ○ 「よい (善)」と「悪い」
   - ○ 「いつも」と「ぜんぜん (今まで一度もない)」

5. 心を落ち着かせ、声を荒らげたり、人に触ったり暴力を振るったりしない。

6. You can disagree without becoming judgmental. Please see Chapter I and III for general information regarding disagreements. Please also see Chapter IV for examples of how to say "no" under the section, "How to have a good conversation in English."

7. Please don't leave the discussion abruptly. You can say the following, for example, when you want to end the discussion peacefully:

"I enjoyed exchanging viewpoints. I've learned a lot from you."

"Thank you for sharing your views with me. I'm glad we had this conversation."

"This is a very difficult subject. Can we explore this more later?"

"I want to discuss this further but need to go take care of something else now. Let's talk about this more some other time."

The following is an excerpt from *Gilead*, a novel written by Marilynne Robinson. It won the Pulitzer prize for fiction in 2005. It takes the format of a memoir where the main character, John Ames, a pastor who knows his death is near, writes a personal account of his life for his seven-year old son.

..., I would advise you against defensiveness on principle. It precludes the best eventualities along with the worst. ... As I have said, the worst eventualities can have great value as experience. And often enough, when

6. 相手の意見に反対するとき、独善的にならない。反対意見の述べ方については、第4章の「『ノー』と言うには」(p.195)をご参照ください。

7. 突然議論を打ち切らない。議論を和やかに終わらせたい場合、以下の表現を使ってみてはいかがでしょうか。

「見方の違いを交換できて楽しかった。あなたから多くのことを学びました」

「あなたの意見を教えてくれてありがとうございます。お話できてうれしかったです」

「これは、難しい案件です。また後でお話できますか？」

「この件についてもっと話したいのですが、あいにく他にしなければならないことがあります。また別の時に改めてお話ししましょう」

　以下は、アメリカ人の小説家、マリリン・ロビンソンが2005年にピューリッツァー賞をとった小説『ギリアッド』という本からの抜粋です。主人公の牧師ジョン・エイムズが自分の死期が近づく中、7歳の息子に向けて書いた回顧録の形をとっています。

　「……原則として、防衛的になりすぎないでください。過剰防衛的になると、最悪の結果とともに、最善の結果を除外してしまうことになります。……前にも言いましたが、最悪の結果に、経験上大きな価値があることがあります。そして、自分を守ってい

we think we are protecting ourselves, we are struggling against our rescuer.

I'd like all of us to avoid pushing away the best possible results and the rescuers in our lives, and try to learn and grow through conversation with others.

Challenges for Japanese

At the beginning of this section I wrote, "many Japanese are not sure how they feel or what they think about the wars." Several Japanese have told me during cultural seminars, "I don't know how to answer questions regarding the wars." I asked them, "What would your response be?" Most of them said, "I don't know because we didn't learn it in school." I have to tell you that this answer is not only meaningless, but it is also the worst possible response. As we discussed before, Westerners place much importance on individualism, a traditional value expressed first by Descartes' "I think therefore I am." To them, your reason, "I was not told what to say about the wars," sounds as if you are saying, "I don't have the ability to think." This can be very damaging to your image. You're less likely to be respected for such a response. So, I'd like you to be able to respond in your own way. But first, I'd like to clarify several things so that you'll have the right mindset towards these difficult questions.

るつもりのときに、実は自分の救済者と争っていることが多いのです」

　最善の結果や救済者を自ら追いやってしまうようなことのないよう、そして相手との対話通じて学び、成長できるよう心がけたいものです。

日本人にとっての難題

　「日本人には、戦争に関して自分が何を感じているのか、考えているのかが自覚できていない人が多いのです」と書きました（p.233）。今まで実施した異文化セミナーで「戦争に関する質問にどう答えたらよいかわかりません」と言う日本人が数人いました。「あなたの返答は何でしょう？」という私の問いかけに、「学校で習わなかったのでわかりません」と答えた人がほとんどでした。申し訳ありませんが、この返答は聞き手にとって無意味なだけでなく、あなたにとって最悪の返答だと言わざるを得ません。デカルトが「我思う、故に我あり」と表現した伝統的な価値観である個人主義は、欧米人にとって大切なものです。「戦争についてどう言えばいいのか指示を受けていません」というのは、欧米人の耳には「私には考える能力がありません」と響きます。これは、あなたのイメージに大打撃を与えかねません。このような返答をして相手に尊重されることは、まずないでしょう。ですから、自分なりに返答できるようになっていただきたいのです。しかしその前に、このような難題に取り組む上でよい心がまえができるよう、いくつかの点について明確にしたいと思います。

You're not responsible for the entire nation

Please remember, unless you are or have been the prime minister of Japan, your opinion or comment won't be interpreted as one that represents the entire nation. Your neighbors, colleagues, or friends are interested in your personal views.

Be authentic

I understand there may be some exceptions to this, however, people ask you challenging questions because they think you're intelligent and can handle them. So, their questions can be a sign of respect. So, you're only responsible for yourself, but at the same time, you don't want to damage their respect for you with your own words. Most important is that you need to be comfortable with your words. Please don't say something from a book that you've just read. Let it sink in, and see if you really agree with the author's view. Take time to cultivate your own view, so that whatever you say will be authentic to who you are.

あなたには、日本という国に対しての責任はありません

　あなたが現在、または過去に日本の総理大臣だったのでなければ、あなたの戦争に関する意見や発言が、日本全体を代表するものとして海外で受け取られる心配はありません。あなたの近所の人や同僚、友だちはあなたの個人的な意見に興味があるのです。

自分に正直に

　たいていの場合、戦争に関するような難しい質問をされるということは、あなたが知的で、難題に対応する能力があると思われているからです。ですから、こういった質問は、あなたに対する尊重の表れと考えていいのです。あなたは自分自身にだけ責任を負っているのですが、同時に、自分の言葉で相手からの尊重を損わないようにしたいものです。一番大切なのは、自分の発言に違和感がないことです。読んだばかりの本の言葉をそのままくり返すようなことはなさらないでください。じっくり読み解き、著者の意見に本当に賛成できるかどうか考えてください。時間をかけて、ご自分の見方を探ってください。そうすることで、あなたの発言が本物になります。

They don't mean to accuse you for Japan's military actions during the wars

Some people ask you about the wars, partly because they assume it's already become a safe subject to talk about. It's been more than seventy years since the Second World War ended. For most people, especially for Westerners who focus on the present and future, seventy years is a very long time. So, it's a surprise for them to learn that the Japanese government doesn't provide much education about the wars, and that some Japanese haven't really reflected on their last wars. Please know that their intentions are not to hurt you or to make you uncomfortable.

How to grapple with questions about Japan's wars

For Japanese who live overseas, December can be an uncomfortable time. Pearl Harbor took place on December 7, 1941 in the U.S. And naturally, many documentary films and TV programs are shown on TV and online. And people stimulated by these programs may ask you questions about Pearl Harbor. They may explain their position on why the U.S. needed to use atomic bombs to end the war. There are many aspects involved in the events that occurred between

彼らには、戦争当時の日本軍の行動に対して、あなたを責める つもりはありません

　戦争の話題はすでに安全な話題になっているはずだと考えて、戦争について聞いてくる欧米の人もいます。第二次世界大戦が終結してから、すでに70年以上経過しています。ほとんどの人、特に現在と未来に注目している欧米人にとって、70年はとても長い年月です。ですから、日本政府が戦争に関する十分な歴史教育を行っていないこと、そして、日本人が自国の最後の戦争についてじっくり考えたことがないのは、欧米人にとっては驚きです。彼らの意図は、あなたを傷つけたり気分を悪くさせようというものではない、ということを知っておいてください。

日本の戦争に関する質問にどう取り組むか

　海外で暮らす日本人にとって、12月は居心地の悪いものです。真珠湾攻撃はアメリカ時間の1941年12月7日に起こりました。戦争関連の多くのドキュメンタリーがテレビやオンラインで映し出されます。これらの番組に刺激を受けた人が、真珠湾攻撃に関して質問してくるかもしれません。中には、どうしてアメリカが戦争を終結させるために原子爆弾を使わなければならなかったかについて、自分の見解を説明する人もいます。真珠湾攻撃と日本の敗戦の間の事態にはさまざまな側面があるので、それぞれ

Pearl Harbor and the end of the war in 1945, so there are many viewpoints and opinions depending on how you look at each development and its backdrop.

Suppose you have done some research on the subject and learned some things. For example, according to some reports, the U.S. government knew of the Japanese military's plan to attack the Pearl Harbor. But the U.S. needed a pretext for going to war; therefore they decided not to defend Hawaii. Some also say that the U.S. needed to justify the enormous amount of investment in developing the atomic bombs. So, they decided to drop the second atomic bomb in Nagasaki, although it was not necessary to end the war.

Suppose one of your friends asks you about the Pearl Harbor attack. I'd like you to consider three things before you mention your new findings.

1) Does such information justify the Pearl Harbor attack?
2) Is it a good time and place to share the results of your research? Do you have a good enough relationship with the inquirer? Is there a risk of being misunderstood?

And most importantly,

3) Are you defensive? Do you feel threatened or criticized?

の局面とその背景をどう見るかによって、見解や意見が違ってきます。

　自分なりに調べてみて、何かを学んだとしましょう。たとえば、当時のアメリカ政府は日本軍の真珠湾攻撃を事前に察知していたという報告書の存在を知ったとします。アメリカは参戦へのきっかけが必要だったので、ハワイを防衛しないことにしました。また、アメリカは核爆弾の開発にかけた巨大な投資を正当化する必要があったとも書いてありました。それが、戦争終結には必要のなかった、2基目の弾頭を長崎に落とすことにした理由だというのです。

　あなたの友だちが真珠湾攻撃について尋ねたとしましょう。あなたが新しく学んだことを言う前に、次の三つのことを考えていただきたいのです。

1）報告書の中の情報が、真珠湾攻撃を正当化するか？
2）あなたの調査結果を知らせるのにいいタイミングと場所かどうか？　質問をした人と、そのような情報を共有するだけの人間関係を築けているか？　誤解を生む可能性があるか？

　そして、もっとも重要な点は

3）過度に防衛的になってないか？　相手に追い詰められたり非難されていると感じていないか？

If your answer to this question is yes, you may decide not to share your findings even when you can say "Yes" to the other two. When you're defensive, you tend to become combative. And it may cause a tit-for-tat argument.

We want to create positive results through conversation. To save the world, to save someone's life, to improve our health, to improve our work environment, to create a better flow of information, to understand others better, to have fun, and so forth. So, when we can't expect a good result, we should be careful about what to share and how.

If we want to be a part of the global community, we should consider another aspect of war: Japan committed many atrocities in Asia. Because the war ended with two atomic bombs, we tend to take a victim's position about the Second World War, however, many people in Asia were killed or injured because of Japan's military actions. As we all know, this still causes anti-Japanese sentiment throughout Asia. Although we don't have to feel that we're personally responsible for the past wars, we should all learn more about how people in Asia experienced the wars.

How will you respond to the question, "What do you think of the last war?"

When a Japanese says to me that he/she doesn't know how to respond to a war-related question because of lack of education, I push back by asking, "Can you share your own opinion or feelings? There is no right or wrong here." I've

もし３の質問に対する答えが「はい」の場合、１、２が「はい」だったとしても、学んだ内容を共有しないほうがいいでしょう。自己防衛に走っていると、けんか腰になりがちです。そして、「目には目を歯には歯を」的な口論になりかねません。

　対話を通してよい結果にたどり着きたいものです。世界を救う、誰かの命を助ける、健康状態の改善、職場環境の改善、情報の流れの改善、相手をよりよく理解する、楽しむなどです。ですから、よい結果が期待できないときは、話題の選択と、どう伝えるかについて注意する必要があります。

　グローバル・コミュニティの一員でありたいのであれば、もう一つ、戦争について考慮すべき点があります。日本はアジアの各地で残虐行為をしました。戦争が核爆弾の投下で終結したので、第二次世界大戦について、私たちは犠牲者の立場をとりがちですが、多くのアジア人が日本軍の軍事行動のせいで亡くなったり負傷したりしました。みなさんがご存じのように、このことが今でもアジアでの反日感情の引き金となっています。今、私たちが過去の戦争に対して個人的に責任を感じる必要はありませんが、アジアの人の戦争体験についてもっと学ぶ必要があります。

　「第二次世界大戦についてどう思いますか？」という質問に、どう答えますか？
　「戦争に関する教育を受けなかったので、質問にどう対応すればよいかわからない」と言う日本人がいると、私は「ご自分なりのご意見やお気持ちを話してもらえますか？　ご意見に正解も誤答もありません」と返します。以下は、いままでに聞いた彼らのコ

heard the following comments:

> "I don't know why people ask such questions."

> "I feel sad about it. It was such a tragedy."

> "I hope Japan will never go down that road."

> "We should monitor carefully what our government is doing."

I can't recommend the first comment as it sounds defensive. But the other responses provide a good starting point. You may want to explain why you think or feel that way.

When you go global, you want to connect with other people as a fellow human being, by mentally going beyond the nation's border. There's no nation on earth that has never experienced wars. But not knowing our own history—especially recent history—may come across to people outside Japan as though we're not equipped with a sense of history or the courage to face our own history. So, I hope we'll all learn more about our history in the 1900s. I also hope we'll have more courage to have difficult conversations among ourselves and with people from other parts of the world.

メントです。

　「どうしてそんな質問をしてくるのかわかりません」

　「悲しいです。本当に悲惨なことです」

　「日本が二度とそのような道を選ばないよう願っています」

　「政府が何をしているのか、注意して見守るべきです」

　一番最初のコメントは、過剰防衛的に聞こえるのでおすすめできません。しかし、他のコメントは、対話のよい出発点だと思います。あながたそう考えたり感じたりしている理由を説明すると、さらによいと思います。

　世界の人と一緒に仕事をしたり遊んだりするとき、心の中で国境を越えて、その人たちと同じ人間としてつながりたいものです。戦争を経験したことのない国はありません。しかし、自分の国の歴史、特に最近の歴史を知らないと、海外の人たちからすると、日本人には歴史観が欠落しているとか、自国の歴史に対峙する勇気がないと思われてしまいます。ですから、私たちが20世紀の歴史をもっと学ぶようになることを願っています。また、私たちが日本人どうしで、また海外の人たちとも、難しい話題について話し合う勇気をもっと持つようになることを願っています。

❖ Summary ❖

Decrease Japanese culture's influence on your English, and develop your global English.

To understand each other is the primary purpose of communication. Let's make your point clear to your counterparts.

There are things that seem natural to Japanese but that would cause bewilderment to non-Japanese.

When you sense you're becoming defensive, avoid reacting quickly, pause and stay calm as you deal with the situation.

Let's try the following:

· Use Action-verbs when you write or speak.

· When possible, use verbs other than "think."

· Select some challenging topics and write your own opinions about them. For example, "what is your religion" "What do you think about Japan's past wars?"

日本文化の影響を減らし、あなたの英語をグローバルな英語に進化させよう。

お互いを理解し合うのがコミュニケーションの目的。ポイントが明確に伝わるようにしよう。

日本人にとっては当たり前でも、海外の人にとっては不思議なこともある。

過剰防衛的になっていると感じたら、反射的な応答を避け、平静な対応をしよう。

やってみよう

・アクション動詞を使って書き、話そう。

・"Think" 以外の動詞を使って、あなたの気持ちや考えを表現しよう。

・難しい話題をいくつか選んで、それに対する自分の見解を書いてみよう。たとえば、「あなたの宗教は何ですか？」「過去の戦争についてどう思うか？」について書いてみよう。

Chapter VI

How to Learn to Speak English

Recently, I found an old book on my bookshelf. I have many bad habits; reading a book that I was going to throw away is one of them. In it, the Japanese author said, if you want to learn English, first you need to read well; next, learn how to listen; and then finally try to learn how to speak. I believe that most Japanese followed her method, which is similar to the Japanese school curriculum, but we didn't become proficient in English. So, although that method worked for her, I have to say that the success of this method remains a myth for the majority of Japanese. Whenever I meet a Japanese who can carry good conversation in English, I ask how they studied. This is the result of my informal research on this subject. They learned it in the following sequence

第6章

英語を話せるようになる勉強方法

　最近、ずいぶん前に買った本が本棚にあるのを見つけました。私には、悪い癖がいろいろありますが、捨てるつもりの本をつい読んでしまうのもその一つです。その本の中で、日本人の著者がこう言っています。「もし英語を学びたいのなら、まず、ちゃんと読めなければならない。次に、聞き取りを学びなさい。そして、最後に話し方を学ぶのです」私が思うに、日本人のほとんどがこの方式——日本の学校の英語の授業に似ています——に従って勉強しましたが、用事を十分足せる英語力は身につきませんでした。ですから、著者に成果をもたらしたこの方式の確実性は、多くの日本人にとって神秘のベールに包まれていると言わざるを得ません。アメリカに来て以来、私は英語の対話能力をお持ちの日本人に会うたびに、どうやって勉強されたのか聞いてきました。これは、私の非正式な調査の結果です。彼らは、以下の順序で学びました。

1. Started talking
2. Learned how to be a good listener
3. Learned how to write
4. Read English articles

In other words, they didn't wait until they felt ready or confident. They were in a situation where they had to or wanted to speak in English, so they did. Also, if you want to be a good listener, you need to speak—more specifically, asking questions. While this may seem to be a paradox, if you can't ask questions when you are not sure, then you will not understand the points that your conversation partners are making. Therefore, some may conclude that "you didn't listen well." So, you need to develop the skills of asking questions. If you can't speak up or ask questions at the right time, you can't improve your listening skills, as these two go hand-in-hand. And in my personal experience, I've found that if I can speak or pronounce the word and phrase (not just know them), then I can understand them right away when I hear them. So, when it comes to conversational skills, learning to speak (and pronounce words correctly) has to come first. Learning English is no different from learning piano or tennis or other activity that involves any part of your body. No matter how many books you've read about them, if you don't play, you can't learn.

1. 話し始め

2. よい聞き手になり

3. 書き方を学び

4. 英語の記事を読んだ

　つまり、準備できた、または自信があると感じるまで待たず、その前に話し始めました。英語を話さざるを得ない、または話したい状況に置かれ、話したのです。また、よい聞き手になりたければ話す、具体的に言うと、質問をしなければなりません。これは逆説に思えるかもしれませんが、聞いた内容がはっきりわからないときに質問できなければ、相手が伝えようとしているポイントを理解できません。結果的に、話し相手の中には「あなたがちゃんと聞かなかった」と判断する人もでてきます。ですから、聞く力を向上させるには、質問するスキルを身につける必要があります。タイミングよく話したり、質問したりしないと、話す力と聞く力は連動しているので、聞く力も向上しません。また、私の個人的な経験では、単語やフレーズを単に知っているだけでなく、話したり発音できる場合は、そういった単語やフレーズを聞いた瞬間に意味を把握できます。対話のスキルを向上させるには、話し方を学ぶ（単語も正しく発音する）ことが一番です。英語を学ぶのは、ピアノやテニス、その他の体を使う活動を学ぶのと何ら変わりありません。どんなにたくさん本を読んでも、実際にプレーしなければ身につきません。

Start talking

So, how to start practicing "Start talking"? This is the process I would recommend.

Step 1: Find something you want to say

Step 2: Think about how to say it

Step 3: Say it, even if you don't know how

Step 4: Learn how to say it better

Go back to step 1.

If you follow these steps, you may not look cool at first. But you'll make a connection with others. Also, they'll know you have something to say. Then, the next cycle (Step 1 through Step 4) becomes a bit easier and faster, because you'll be less anxious.

The most important step is Step 3 (Say it, even if you don't know how). I can't overemphasize its importance. And this is the most challenging part for Japanese, because we tend to worry about how others see us. So, you need to focus on your purpose and goal (what you want to convey and why), rather than how you look to others. And please remember to keep talking for at least three sentences. If your first sentence doesn't help them understand your intention, don't be discouraged. With your second and third sentences, they may

話し始める

　では、どうやって「話し始める」練習をすればいいのでしょう？
以下は私がおすすめする方法です。

　　ステップ 1:　何か言いたいことを見つけ

　　ステップ 2:　どう言うか考える

　　ステップ 3:　言い方がわからなくても、話す

　　ステップ 4:　もっとよい言い方を学ぶ

　　1に戻ってくり返す

　このステップを実行すると、最初は格好よくありません。しか
し、相手と知り合うことができます。また、あなたには言いたい
ことがあるとわかってもらえます。そうすると次のサイクルのと
き（ステップ１から４）、最初のときに比べると不安が少ないの
で、ステップ１から４を簡単に早くこなせるようになります。
　一番大切なステップは３（言い方がわからなくても、話す）で
す。この段階の大切さは言い尽くせません。そして、これが人に
どう見られているかを気にする日本人にとっては、一番難しいと
ころです。人の目にどう映るかではなく、あなたの目的と目標（何
を言いたいのか、その理由は何か）を中心に考えてください。そ
して、３文は必ず話し続けることを、どうぞお忘れなく。最初の
文であなたの意図を相手に伝えられなくても、がっかりしないで
ください。２文目か３文目で、あなたが話した理由をわかっても
らえ、役立つ情報を教えてもらえるかもしれません。

get the idea of why you spoke up, and then provide you with information that could be helpful to you.

Let's say you didn't speak well today. Please be assured that you still did a great service to yourself. We can't underestimate human ability; we are intuitive and can sense when someone knows something or is willing to share his/her own view. By speaking up, you can raise other people's interest in you. This will help you cultivate relationships with others through English conversation. Let's make the nature of human curiosity work for you.

In other words, being silent is the worst thing you can do to yourself. Some Westerners will misunderstand your modesty and silence, and some may think that you're hiding something. This is not good PR. Besides, especially in the U.S., people appreciate others who try hard. So, let's keep trying.

I understand, though, that following these steps can be very challenging. One way to deal with this is to take time going through the process. For example, you can tackle Step 1 on your way home from work, or while you're taking a shower. The next morning, you can write down some English sentences in your notebook while you're on the train. Then, when you get a chance to talk, even if you're not ready, tell them anyway. Although it didn't sound right or great, you're most likely halfway there. 50 percent is a lot better than nothing! Practice makes perfect. You'll soon find yourself going through this cycle many times in a meeting or a conversation over coffee.

今日はうまく話せなかったとしましょう。それでも、あなたは自分自身のためになることをしたのです。人間の能力を過小評価することはできません。私たち人間には直観的な知覚能力があって、誰かが何か大事なことを知っていたり、意見を共有しようとしていると、それを感知します。進んで話すことで、相手はあなたにもっと興味を持ちます。これは英語の対話を通じて人間関係を築くのにとても役立ちます。人間が本来持っている好奇心に訴え、その効果を生かしましょう。

　言い換えると、沈黙があなたに一番不利な状況を生むのです。欧米人の中には、あなたの謙虚さと沈黙を誤解する人もいますし、あなたが何かを隠していると思う人もいるかもしれません。沈黙は、よいPRにはなりません。また特にアメリカでは、一生懸命頑張る人が評価されます。ですから、ぜひ頑張って話し続けてください。

　これらのステップをこなすのは大変なことだというのは、私もわかっています。これに対応する一つの方法は、全体の過程（4つのステップ）に時間をかけて取り組むことです。たとえば、ステップ1について、仕事からの帰宅途中やシャワー中に取り組みます。次の朝、電車に乗っている間に、英文をメモします。そして、話すチャンスがまわってきたら、まだ十分準備ができていなくとも、とにかく話してみるのです。きちんと話せなかったり、思い通りにいかなかったとしても、たいていの場合、半分はできています。50%はゼロよりずっといいです！　練習を積み重ねることで、上手くなっていくのです。ほどなく、このサイクルを会議中やコーヒーを飲みながらの対話の中で、何度もくり返している自分に気づくはずです。

If you feel you're not making progress, and you know a native speaker of English, ask for help. That'll be a very good small talk subject; they'll know what is difficult for you, and they will understand that you're trying.

We already discussed the importance of making your point quickly in Chapter I, "Message (Melody)." In many cases, after you've made your point, you may want to explain what happened before in order to show why you're making a request, asking a question, or making a comment. Therefore, I'd like you to practice talking in the past tense.

■ Practice [1]

Practice talking in the past tense

This seems easy. We all learned the past form of "give" is "gave," for instance. But when you need to speak, you may find it hard to pull out the word "gave" from your brain. The only way to improve your brain-mouth connection is practice. Practice makes your brain-mouth connection shorter, and eventually automatic.

"I'm afraid I can't join you for lunch. We <u>received</u> new information that <u>led</u> us to reconsider our position."

"I'd like a replacement for this product. I <u>bought</u> this last Wednesday, but it <u>didn't</u> work."

"I want to discuss scheduling again. You <u>brought</u> up an important point in our last discussion."

なかなか上達しないと感じていて、英語を話す人が身近にいる場合、助けを求めてください。これは、世間話に恰好の話題です。あなたがどこでつまずいているのかわかってもらえますし、あなたが頑張っていることも認めてもらえます。

自分の一番言いたいことを早く言うことの大切さを、第1章の「7つの要素[2]メッセージ——メロディ」（p.49）で書きました。多くの場合、一番大事なポイントを伝えたあと、前にどんなことが起こったのかを説明し、あなたのお願いや質問、発言の理由をわかってもらおうとするでしょう。ですから、次のように話す練習をしていただきたいのです。

■練習[1]

過去形で話す練習

簡単に思えるかもしれません。たとえば「give」の過去形が「gave」だというのは学校で習いました。けれども、話している最中に「gave」を頭からひっぱりだしてくるのは、なかなか難しいです。この頭と口の連携を向上させる唯一の方法は練習です。練習することで、頭と口の連携時間が短縮され、そのうち自動的にできるようになります。

「残念ですが、ランチをご一緒できません。新しい情報を受け取り、私たちの立場の再考が必要になりました」

「この製品の引換をお願いします。先週の水曜日に買ったのですが、動きません」

「日程についてもう一度話したいです。前回の討議で、あなたは重要なポイントを提示してくれました」

"The project is going well now. The additional manpower brought immediate relief to our department."

"I've been thinking about new approaches. His comments from our last meeting gave me several ideas."

"Your situation sounds similar to something that I've experienced before. So, I thought I'd (I would) share my experience with you."

The present perfect tense

Once you've become comfortable talking in the past tense, then start tackling the present perfect tense. This is a little tricky, probably because in Japanese we call it 現在完了形. This may give you an impression that something needs to be completed. But that is not always the case. We can use the present perfect for things that have been going on for a long time, and which we don't expect to end any time soon.

"I've been learning tea ceremony for three years."

"I've been thinking about going to Greece since I was in middle school."

"Compensation issues have been giving me headaches for many years."

If you can use the present perfect tense, your conversation becomes livelier. The past is behind us and most Westerners

「プロジェクトは順調に進行しています。人員を追加したことで、我が部署はすぐ落ち着きました」

「新しいやり方を考えてきました。前回の会議で彼の発言を聞いて、いろんなアイデアが浮かびました」

「あなたの状況は、私が前に経験したものに似ているようです。ですから、私の経験をお話ししようと思ったのです」

現在完了形

　過去形で話すのに慣れたら、今度は現在完了形に挑戦してみましょう。これは、少々ややこしいです。これはおそらく、私たちがこの時制を「現在完了形」と呼ぶからだと思います。この訳のおかげで、何かが完了しないといけないという印象を受けるのかもしれません。しかし、いつもそうだとは限りません。現在完了形は、長い間起こっていることで、すぐには終わらないことについても使えます。

　「茶道を３年間習っています」

　「中学生のときから、ギリシャに行きたいと思っています」

　「給与の案件は、長年頭痛の種です」

　現在完了形を使えるようになると、対話が生き生きとしてきます。過去はすでに過ぎ去ったことで、欧米人の多くは過去のこと

are not particularly interested in the past. But sentences in the present perfect tense reside in the present. It signals that you're talking about something that is happening now, that has been going on until now, or has just been completed. This catches other people's attention.

I'd like to add one more point. Grammatically speaking, you cannot use a word that suggests the "past" in the present perfect sentence. For example, strictly speaking, "I've just met Sarah two minutes ago," is incorrect. Whether two minutes ago or two days ago, it belongs to the past. You may want to use "recently" instead of "yesterday," as the adverb "recently" belongs to the present tense. Or you can speak in the past tense: I saw him yesterday.

One of my friends pointed out that when a train is coming to the station, Japanese tend to say, "The train has come," in present perfect tense. However, native speakers of English would say, "The train is coming." This is an interesting point when we think about how each culture sees time and space differently and how "seeing and recognizing an object" for Japanese is connected with our sense of time: if you see it, it's already here.

■ Practice [3]
Subjunctive mood

When you're comfortable, start trying to use the subjunctive

にはあまり興味がありません。しかし、現在完了形の文は現在に属します。現在完了形を使うと、過去から現在にまで引き続き起こり、現在も起こっていること、もしくは完了したばかりの物事について話していることを示せます。それで、話し相手の注目を引きやすいのです。

　もう一点、ポイントを追加させてください。文法的には、現在完了形の文には「過去」を思わせる単語を使えません。たとえば、厳密に言うと、「2分前にサラに会った（現在完了形の文）」は間違いです。2分前であれ、2日前であれ、過去に属します。副詞のrecently（最近）は現在に属するので、"I've seen Sarah recently."と言えます。しかし、"I've seen Sarah yesterday." は間違いです。文全体を過去形にして "I saw Sarah yesterday." としてください。

　友人の一人が教えてくれたのですが、電車が駅に向かって来ているとき、日本人はたいてい「電車が来た」と現在完了形で話します。しかし、ネイティブ・スピーカーは「電車が来ている」と現在進行形で話します。これは、それぞれの文化で時間と空間の知覚のしかたが違うこと、また日本人の「物体を見て認識する」しかたが、時間の感覚と関連している（見えたら、もう来たと同じ）ことを考えると、興味深いです。

■練習 [3]
仮定法

　できそうだなと感じたら、仮定法を使い始めてください。これ

mood. This will make your English sound much more sophisticated. You don't need to go back to your old grammar book. Just remember a few phrases that are useful for you.

The following sentences can be used to express your message politely:

"If I were you, I would avoid that type of situation."
 * "If I was you …" is now also considered grammatically correct in the U.S.

"I'd appreciate it if you could get back to me by tomorrow morning."

The following two sentences express something didn't happen, which you feel sorry about:

"I'm sorry, I should've thought about it before."

"We should've caught it, but unfortunately, we didn't see it coming."

Learn how to be a good listener

■Listening Skills [1]
Timing is everything

Westerners assume that if you're a good listener, you will ask questions. In other words, if you don't ask any questions for a period of time, they may think that you are not engaged

が使いこなせると、あなたの英語がぐっと上品に響きます。古い文法書を引っ張り出してくる必要がありません。使いでのあるフレーズをいくつか覚えれば十分です。

　以下の文を使うと、言いたいことを丁寧に伝えることができます。

　　「私だったら、そんな状況を避けます」
　　　＊ "If I was you ..." も今はアメリカでは正しいとされています。

　　「明日の朝までに連絡してくれると、ありがたいです」

　次の文は、何かが起こらず残念だったという気持ちを表現します。

　　「すみません。それを前に考えるべきでした」
　　「気づくべきでしたが、残念ながら予想もしていませんでした」

よい聞き手になるには

■ よい聞き手とは [1]
タイミングが大事

　欧米人は、あなたが注意深く聞いていれば、質問をしてくるだろうと思っています。つまり、長い間質問しないでいると、あなたが対話に聞き入っていなかったと思うのです。ですから最初に

in the conversation. The first thing you need to do is memorize some useful questions, so that you can ask those questions when you get a "?" in your head. Please see the "How to have more air time" section in Chapter II for examples. And remember that the timing for you to say "Excuse me!" is equally or even more important than what you're going to say next. If you can't compose a specific question right away, then you may want to say, "I don't think I understand what you've said. Can you explain it again, please?"

■ Listening Skills [2]

Be clear on yes or no, and consider taking the "yes" side

You may have heard the advice many times that "you need to be clear about yes or no when speaking English." Although this is a good piece of advice, many Japanese are too hesitant to say "yes" when they have even minor questions or reservations. And this doesn't work very well for Japanese, as Westerners may see us closed-minded. Please note that saying "yes" to something doesn't mean that you can't ask questions to make things clear to you. Just accept that nothing can be perfect at least initially. And if you're 80 percent okay with an idea or proposal, I'd recommend that you'd take the position of "yes."

I'm an advocate of the "yes and yes" approach in English conversation. The "yes and but" approach tends to give

していただきたいのは、いくつか使えそうな質問を暗記して、頭の中に「？」が浮かんだら、すぐに質問することです。第2章の「もっと長く話す」（p.115）をご参照ください。そして、肝に銘じていただきたいのは、「すみません！（Excuse me!）」というタイミングが、それに続く発言と同じぐらい、またはそれ以上に大切だということです。具体的な質問をすぐ投げかけられない場合、「あなたのおっしゃったことがよくわかりません。もう一度説明していただけますか？」と言うのがよいでしょう。

■よい聞き手とは［2］
イエスかノーを明確に、そしてなるべく「イエス」で応じる

「英語で話すときはイエスかノーを明確に」というアドバイスを聞いたことがあると思います。これはよいアドバイスですが、日本人は往々にして、ほんの少しでも疑問点や迷いがあると、「イエス」と言うのをためらいます。残念ながら、欧米人はこのような態度を狭量さの表れと見るので、日本人にとってよいことはありません。「イエス」と言っても、質問して物事を明確にできないわけではありません。一回で物事が完璧になることはないということを、受け入れてください。もしアイデアや提案を80％受け入れられるのであれば、「イエス」の立場を取ることをおすすめします。

私は、英語の対話では「yesとyes」のアプローチを提唱しています。「yesとbut」のアプローチは、あなたが次に述べるポイントが堂々巡りをして、議論が進んでいるときも停滞しているよう

Westerners an impression that the points you make next will go in circles, and that the discussion is not progressing forward, even when it is. Please compare the following examples:

Example A

Yes and Yes: "I agree that Wednesday would be the best day for this. Next, we need to think about which restaurant will be best for the occasion."

Yes and But: "I agree that Wednesday would be the best day for this. But we need to make sure that we pick a restaurant that is appropriate for the occasion."

Example B

Yes and Yes: "Yes, I agree on your approach. How can we make it happen? Have you thought about the budget to get it going?"

Yes and But: "I agree on your approach. But can you make it happen? I'm concerned about the budget to get it going."

For other listening techniques, please see Chapter III: Small Talk.

▪ Listening Skills [3]

Practice listening with a focus on speaking

When I came to the U.S., I couldn't speak a word of English. Well, that's an exaggeration, but the only words that I could

な印象を欧米人に与えてしまいます。以下の例をご覧ください。

例 A

Yes と Yes: 「私もこれには水曜日が一番よい日だと思います。
　　　　　　次に、どのレストランが一番相応しいか、考えな
　　　　　　ければなりません」

Yes と But: 「私もこれには水曜日が一番よい日だと思います。
　　　　　　しかし、この場合に相応しいレストランをちゃん
　　　　　　と選ばなければなりません」

例 B

Yes と Yes: 「あなたの進め方に賛成です。どうやって実現しま
　　　　　　すか？ 作業を始めるための予算について考えまし
　　　　　　たか？」

Yes と But: 「あなたの取り組み方に賛成です。しかし、実現で
　　　　　　きますか？ 作業開始の予算について心配していま
　　　　　　す」

その他のテクニックについては、第3章「スモールトーク（世間話）」（p.127）を参照してください。

■よい聞き手とは［3］

話すことを念頭に置いて、聞く練習をする

アメリカに来たとき、私は英語を一言も話せませんでした。それは少し大げさですが、考えずに言える英語は「ありがとう」と

say without thinking were "Thank you," "yes," and "no." I still remember the first English phrase that I learned was "No, thank you." When you decline an offer, whether it's a drink or a chair to sit, please say "No, thank you." When you accept an offer, say "Yes, please."

The first thing I did to learn English was to watch a TV series called Star Trek. I collected and memorized short English sentences that I heard. If you're interested in learning how to manage a global business with diverse cultures, you can also learn some things from this TV series.

Later, I also collected and memorized English expressions from movies.

Now visual materials are abundant, thanks to the Internet. I find them very helpful, as they give you visual information about the situation, so you can learn the appropriate English expression for a situation.

You can learn new words by doing this; however, my primary focus was to collect short sentences and phrases that I could use the next day. I listened to the conversation in TV programs and movies, in order for me to be able to speak more often and with better phrases. You don't have to create a long and beautiful sentence unless you want to demonstrate your intellectual ability in English. For most of us, knowing and saying enough English expressions is more important, because they'll give us tools to get involved in a conversation or a discussion.

Here are some examples:

「はい」「いいえ」だけでした。最初に学んだ英語表現は、「いいえ、結構です（No, thank you.）」だったのを今も覚えています。それが飲み物であれ、椅子であれ、誰かの申し出を断るときは、No, thank you. と言ってください。申し出を受け入れるときは、「はい、お願いします（Yes, please.）」と言います。

　英語を学ぶために最初にしたのは、テレビ・シリーズの「スタートレック」を見たことでした。聞き取れた短い英語の文を丸覚えしました。もし、多文化環境でのグローバル・ビジネスに興味があれば、このテレビ・シリーズから学べることがいくつかあります。

　その後、映画の中の英語表現も集めて覚えました。

　今はインターネットのおかげで、視覚材料があふれています。状況に関する視覚情報を提供してくれるので、状況に応じた英語表現を学ぶのに役立ちます。

　この方法で語彙を増やすこともできますが、一番の目的は、次の日に使える短い文やフレーズを集めることでした。もっと頻繁に自然なフレーズで話せるよう、テレビや映画の中の会話を聞きました。英語であなたの知性を披露したいのでなければ、長く美しい文を話す必要はありません。ほとんどの人にとっては、十分な量の英語表現を知り、言えることのほうが大事です。使える英語表現が十分あれば、対話や討議に参加しやすくなります。

　以下はその例です。

"Don't even think about it."

"I was taken by surprise."

"It never occurred to me."

"It has been brought to my attention."

"Have a good Fourth!" (*July 4th is America's Independence Day)

Learn how to write

■ Writing Skills [1]
Know that you have a good foundation for writing

First, I need to emphasize the fact that if you graduated from middle school, you know enough English words to compose a good and functional email or a letter. You can see how little vocabulary I use in this book. You can explain a complicated matter using basic vocabulary. Of course, if you have a larger vocabulary, you can convey your message in a more nuanced way. So, please keep learning and writing. But please know that you already have a good foundation. You may just have to jog your memory

■ Writing Skills [2]
Apologies can get lost in translation

We've been discussing how to communicate clearly in English so that we can build better relationships with

「そんなこと考えたらだめよ」

「びっくりしました」

「考えもつきませんでした」

「ついさきほど知りました」

「楽しい7月4日を！」(＊この日はアメリカの独立記念日です)

書き方を学ぶ

■ よい書き手とは [1]

英語で書くための基礎は十分ある

　まず、あなたが中学校を出たのであれば、用事をこなすための
電子メールや手紙を書くには十分な英語力があります。私がこの
本で使っている語彙は、非常に限られています。もちろん、語彙
をたくさんお持ちであれば、より細かなニュアンスを伝えること
ができます。ですから、学び続け、書き続けてください。しかし、
あなたには基礎が十分あることをわかっていただきたいのです。
昔習った英語の記憶を呼び戻せばいいのです。

■ よい書き手とは [2]

陳謝が招くズレ

　ここまでずっと話してきたのは、海外の人とよりよい人間関係
を築くために、どうやって英語で明確にコミュニケートするかで

non-Japanese. I'd like to share one more "lost in translation" case here. This is a real-life example of an email exchange. Several emails were exchanged between two Americans. One of them is my teenage daughter.

⟨ My daughter's email to Mr. White ⟩

Hi Mr. White!

I'm so sorry this is last minute, but I just realized I have to babysit from 5 pm this Saturday, November 18th. Our meeting this Saturday goes from 4 to 5, and it takes twenty minutes to drive back home. I'm really sorry, but the parents I'm babysitting for have to go to a wedding, so I don't think I can ask them to let me come late. Are you available any time tomorrow, Wednesday November 15th? I'm really really sorry this is last minute.

Additionally, what days are you available during the month of December?

Thank you and sorry again,
Yuki Schwab

⟨ Mr. White's response ⟩

Yuki —

Please no apologies. You are amazing, and you are handling this scheduling issue with aplomb (doing it with confidence in a relaxed way). The notice is well timed and thorough.

I am completely full during the week but what about

す。ここで、もう一つ「翻訳のズレ」の例を紹介します。これは、実際に起こったEメールのやり取りで、数通のメールが二人のアメリカ人の間で交換されました。そのうちの一人は、私の十代の娘です。

〈娘からホワイトさんへのメール〉

> ホワイトさん！
> 直前で申し訳ないのですが。今週の土曜、11月18日の5時から子守をしなければならないことに気づきました。私たちのミーティングは土曜の4時から5時に設定されていて、お宅から自宅に戻るのに車で20分かかります。本当にすみませんが、私の雇い主はその日、結婚式に行かねばならず、私の到着が遅れるわけにはいきません。明日の水曜日、11月15日にお時間ありますか？ ぎりぎりになってしまって、本当に本当にすみません。
> それから、12月はどの日のご都合がよいですか？
>
> ありがとうございます。そして、再度すみません。
> ゆき

〈ホワイトさんからの返事〉

> ゆき
> どうか、あやまらないでください。あなたは素晴らしく、この日程の件にうまく対応しています。通知のタイミングはよく、また、内容に漏れがありません。
> 今週の予定は埋まっていますが、日曜日はどうですか？ 空いてる時

Sunday? I have openings then. Also, there is a chance that 3:00 on Saturday will be open.

Send me some possible times for Sunday, and I will confirm my 3:00 on Saturday for you.

Also, it was my understanding that the 4:00 Saturday slot was yours until we change it if we have to. So, let's talk about scheduling when we meet next.

〈 Another response to Mr. White 〉

Mr. White,

Thank you so much, Saturday at 3 would be great! If not, any time on Sunday until 3 pm works well. And sorry about the changes to my original 4 pm Saturday slot. In December, a lot of my piano performances fall on Saturdays and I thought it would be easier to change the times because I also thought the slots were just for the month. Sorry!

Thank you!

Yuki Schwab

〈 Mr. White's advice to Yuki 〉

Yuki —

I will get back to you re: Saturday the 18th. And we'll figure out December. I have some room on Sunday for sure. We'll make it work.

You are a busy, amazing young woman. I encourage you not to apologize but to share your concern for my busy schedule or some such. As you navigate the world of college

間があります。また、土曜日の３時が空く可能性もあります。

日曜日に来られる時間を教えてください。土曜日の３時について
は、私のほうから確認を入れます。

また、私の理解では、変更が必要になるまで、土曜の４時はあなた
のために取ってある時間です。次回のミーティングで、予定につい
て話しましょう。

〈娘からホワイトさんへのメール 2〉

ホワイトさん

ありがとうございます。土曜の３時はありがたいです。この時間の
都合が合わなければ、日曜の３時までならいつでも大丈夫です。も
ともとの土曜の４時の時間を変更することになり、申し訳ありませ
ん。12月にはピアノの発表会が土曜日にあり、また、その時間は
11月だけのものと思っていたので、簡単に変えられると思っていま
した。すみません！

ありがとうございます！

ゆき

〈ホワイトさんからゆきへのアドバイス〉

ゆき

18日 (土) については、あとで連絡します。12月については一緒に
考えましょう。日曜に時間があるのは確実です。なんとか解決でき
ます。

あなたは、忙しく、素晴らしい若い女性です。あやまるかわりに、
私の忙しい日程などについての心配りを示すようにしてください。
大学と仕事の世界で、その小さな調整の価値を実感するでしょう。

and your professional life, that minor adjustment will prove valuable.

I appreciate your flexibility and attention to my busy schedule. It is incumbent (*responsibility) on me to respect your schedule and life, as I do.

Please forgive my forwardness (*boldness, aggressiveness) in giving such advice, but I consider it my obligation. (Notice how I apologized while still asserting confidently that I was correct in offering the advice. You can do the same sort of thing.)

See you soon.

〈 My thank-you note to Mr. White 〉

Thank you, Mr. White. I've been working on it but never made a dent. Yuki is very American, but she is very Japanese when it comes to apologies (she's more apologetic than most Japanese). I truly appreciate your advice for Yuki.

Michiko Schwab

The point that I'd like to convey is this: apologies don't always work in English. Native speakers of English may get confused or feel uncomfortable with Japanese apologies, because they don't apologize in order to be polite. Also, they feel as if they had treated you unfairly, even when they know they didn't. Too much apology can also be seen as a sign of a passive-aggressive (indirect resistance, an avoidance of direct

融通が利く点と私の忙しい日程への気配りには感謝します。あなたの日程と生活を尊重するのは、私にとっても大事なことです。

このようなアドバイスをする差し出がましさを許してください。しかし、これは私の義務と考えます。（私があやまりながらも、このアドバイスを提供することが正しいことだと自信を持って主張している点に注目してください。）

ではまた。

〈私からホワイトさんへの感謝のメール〉

ホワイトさん、ありがとうございます。この点についてはずっと娘に話してきたのですが、少しも変化がありませんでした。ゆきは生粋のアメリカ人ですが、あやまることに関してはとても日本的です（一般の日本人より頻繁にあやまります）。ゆきへのアドバイスに心より感謝いたします。

しゅわぶ美智子

　私がお伝えしたいポイントは、英語でのコミュニケーションでは、謝罪は必ずしも功を奏さないということです。ネイティブスピーカーは礼儀正しさを表現する目的ではあやまらないので、彼らは日本人の謝罪で混乱するか、居心地が悪くなってしまいます。また、自分ではそんなことはしなかったとわかっていても、あなたを理不尽に扱ってしまったかのように感じてしまいます。また、謝罪をしすぎると、あなたは受け身に見せかけた攻撃（間

confrontation) attitude. All of this can result in a less positive impression of you. Of course, we want to apologize when we made a mistake. But otherwise, try to replace 30 percent of your "sorries" with "thank yous." "Thank you for your help!" sounds much better than "I'm sorry for the inconvenience."

Another key lesson from this is that we shouldn't make too much of a fuss about apologies (or rather the lack of them), when non-Japanese didn't apologize when you thought they should have. Instead, we should celebrate that things are moving forward, you're getting closer to a shared goal, the mistakes have been corrected, and that you and your counterpart are still enjoying a good relationship. I know, staying positive sometimes requires a lot of mental effort!

Read English articles (at least) once a week

This is the easiest among the four, however it takes some discipline. Be sure to set some time aside for reading. Please read anything you like. If you read something that interests you, you can use the vocabulary from the article in conversations or small talk. You may even learn something new that you can share with friends or colleagues. In fact, I've been reading an article every weekend for more than twenty-five years. On weekdays, I'm busy with work, and I can't look up every word that I'm not really sure about. For the sake of time, if

接的な抵抗、直接対立の回避)をする人だと思われてしまいます。これらはすべて、あなたの印象を悪くする結果になります。もちろん、間違った場合はあやまるのが当然です。しかし、そうでない場合は、「すみません」の30パーセントを「ありがとう」に変えてください。「手伝ってくれてありがとう」は、「お手数をおかけしてすみません」よりずっとよく響きます。

このメールのやり取りから学べるもう一つの点は、あなたが海外の人があやまるべきだと思ったのにあやまらなかった場合、謝罪(というよりは、むしろ謝罪の欠如)にこだわりすぎないほうがいいということです。それよりも、物事が前進しつつあること、共通の目標に近づきつつあること、間違いが訂正されたこと、相手とあなたがよい人間関係にあることを、ともに喜ぶほうがよいのです。前向きであり続けるには、時として心理的な努力が必要です!

英語の記事を週に最低一つ読む

これは四つのステップの中で一番簡単ですが、習慣づけが必要です。読むための時間を確保してください。内容は何でも好きなものでかまいません。あなたが面白いと思うものを読むと、そこに書かれてある語彙を対話やスモールトークで使えます。友だちや同僚に話したくなるような新しい知識を得るかもしれません。私は25年以上の間、週末に必ず記事を一つ読んでいます。週日は仕事で忙しく、意味が確実でない単語をすべて辞書で調べる時間がありません。時間が惜しいので、記事の趣旨がわかれば、それでよしとします。しかし週末には一つひとつの単語を丹念に読

I get the gist of an article, I'll move on. But on weekends, I read one article word by word, and I'll look up every word if I have the slightest doubt. My purpose is to find errors in my own English, and self-correct it. I've met many Japanese who mistake one word for another. This can cause confusion or misunderstandings. The following are some examples:

He is funny vs. **he is fun**
"**Let's have fun**" is correct,
but "Let's have funny" is not

I'm bored vs. **I'm boring**

Quality product vs. **qualified product**

He means it vs. **He is mean**
"He is meaning" is incorrect

It takes time to improve your English, but reading can help you with speaking, listening, and writing. If you can, please read out loud. Make sure you pronounce each sound clearly, especially the sounds that are not in the Japanese language.

bug and bag
uncle and ankle
van and ban
right and light
wrong and long

み、少しでも自信のない単語は辞書で調べます。この目的は自分の英語の間違いを洗い出し、自分で正すことです。ある単語を別の意味にとってしまっている日本人の方に多く出会います。これは、混乱や誤解のもとです。以下はそんな単語の例です。

「彼は面白い(笑わせてくれる)」vs.「彼は楽しい人だ」
　　○ "Let's have fun."（楽しもう）
　　× "Let's have funny."

「つまらない(飽きた)」vs.「私は面白くない人間だ」

「高品質の製品」vs.「基準に達した製品」

「彼は本気でそう思っている」vs.「彼はいじわるだ」
　　× "He is meaning."

　英語力をつけるのには時間がかかりますが、読むことで、話す力と聞く力、書く力がつきます。できれば、声に出して読んでください。一つひとつの音、特に日本語にない音をはっきり発音するよう心がけてください。

　　bug and bag　　　（虫とバッグ）

　　uncle and ankle　（おじさんと足首）

　　van and ban　　　（車のバンと禁止）

　　right and light　（右/正しいと光/軽い）

　　wrong and long　（間違っていると長い）

One of the things that I'd recommend is that you read books on history or history-related topics and develop your own world view. This is something most Westerners do as they grow up and Japanese don't do enough. And this creates a knowledge gap between Japanese and non-Japanese. More important, not having a point of view on history and the world can be perceived as a weakness outside of Japan. This is not for tests, so what is thought to be right or wrong isn't very important. Curiosity towards fellow humans in the past and humanity in the present are the things that connect us with others around the world. If you've lived in Japan your whole life, you may not feel this way. You'll be pleasantly surprised, if you try.

Here are some books that I enjoyed reading, and helped me think about myself, my family, Japan, and the world through different lenses.

A History of the World in 6 Glasses by Tom Standage

The Only Woman in the Room by Beate Sirota Gordon

Embracing Defeat by John W. Dower

Japan and the Shackles of the Past by R. Taggart Murphy

A Modern History of Japan by Andrew Gordon

Homo Deus by Yuval Noah Harari

Justice by Michael J. Sandel

Seven Brief Lessons on Physics by Carlo Rovelli

もう一つおすすめしたいのは、歴史や歴史関係について書かれた本を読み、自分なりの世界観を作ることです。これは、ほとんどの欧米の子どもたちが成長の過程ですることですが、日本人の子どもたちは十分しないままに育ってしまいます。そしてこれが日本人と海外の人との間に知識の差を生みます。もっと大事なのは、自分なりの歴史観や世界観を持っていないことが、海外では弱点と見られることです。テストのために勉強するわけではありませんから、何が正しく、何が間違いとされているかにこだわる必要はありません。過去を生きた人たち、そして時代を共有する人たちに興味を持つことで、私たちは世界の人たちと心を通わせることができるのです。もし、今まで一歩も日本を出たことがなかったら、こんな風に感じないかもしれません。歴史関係の本を読んだら、意外で楽しい驚きを経験するでしょう。

　　以下は、私が面白いと思った本で、自分や家族、日本、世界について違った角度で考えるよい機会となりました。

『世界を変えた6つの飲み物』　トム・スタンデージ著
『1945年のクリスマス』　ベアテ・シロタ・ゴードン著
『敗北を抱きしめて』　ジョン・ダワー著
『日本——呪縛の構図』　ターガート・マーフィー著
『日本の200年——徳川時代から現代まで』　アンドルー・ゴードン著
『ホモ・デウス』　ユヴァル・ノア・ハラリ著
『これからの「正義」の話をしよう』　マイケル・サンデル著
『Seven Brief Lessons on Physics』　カルロ・ロヴェッリ著

❖ Summary ❖

To start talking in English is the quickest way to improve your conversation skills. Encourage yourself to speak in English, even when you don't know how to say what you want to say.

Master speaking in the past tense.

You need to ask good questions, if you want to become an attentive listener.

If you apologize too often, your conversation partners may come away with an unintended impression: you're too obsequious or have no backbone. Please convey your appreciation by saying "thank you" instead of "sorry."

Connection among individuals is important in the English-speaking world. To make yourself an attractive individual, you need to be aware of your own perspectives and opinions. Discover or construct your view of history and the world.

とにかく話し始めるのが英語の対話を上達させる早道。言い方がわからなくても、勇気をだして話し始めよう。

過去形を使いこなそう。

質問をして、よい聞き手になろう。

英語で頻繁に謝罪すると、卑屈な人だという思いもよらない印象を与えてしまうこともある。感謝の気持ちは"sorry"よりも"thank you"で伝えよう。

英語の世界は個人と個人のつながりが大切。個人としてのあなたに興味を持ってもらうには、自分の見方や考え方を自覚していることが大切。自分の歴史観や世界観を持とう／発見しよう。

Let's try the following:

- Success is built on failure. Avoid becoming tense by thinking you need to speak perfect English. Summon courage and jump into conversation.

- Summarize your thoughts in easy English before meetings.

- Practice telling stories in the past tense.

- Recollect your own examples where you responded by "yes, but …" and rephrase them using a more positive "yes and a question" pattern.

- Daily efforts will bear fruit. Keep writing what you want to say or reading English articles. Doing it for only three days at a time is totally acceptable. Be sure to start again. Persistence pays off.

- Read history books written in English. It is still effective if you read only the parts in the book that you're interested. You could start reading about the history of baseball, cooking or anything that would be of interest.

やってみよう

・失敗は成功のもと。正しい英語を話そうと固くならず、勇気を
　もって対話に飛び込んでみよう。

・ミーティングの前などに、自分の考えを簡単な英語で書き留め
　ておく。

・過去形で話し続ける練習をしよう。

・"Yes, but ..."で対応した例を思い出し、前向きな「Yes と質
　問」に変えて、英作文してみよう。

・日常的な努力が実を結ぶ。言いたいことを書いてみる、英語の
　記事を読むなどの努力を継続しよう。三日坊主でもよし。三日
　坊主をくり返せば、チリも積もる。

・英語で書かれた歴史書を読んでみよう。興味のあるところを拾
　い読みするだけでも効果あり。野球の歴史、料理の歴史など、
　あなたが興味のあるところをきっかけにされてはいかが？

IMHO *(In My Humble Opinion)*

I wanted to send my fellow Japanese a message, but I wasn't able to include it in an earlier chapter as it's a rather personal message. So, in place of an end note, I'd like to write my "IMHO" (In My Humble Opinion).

When I started working as an intercultural trainer/coach more than twenty years ago, I thought my work would disappear. Japanese would be exposed to and be connected with the world and would become a more integrated part of the world. Indeed, across business, volunteer activities, and daily life, I have met many Japanese who have the courage to get into the global field and are making great contributions by utilizing their knowledge, skills, and wisdom.

However, I've also seen another trend with many other Japanese, especially after the 2008 global financial crisis. Some Japanese have become extremely risk-averse (afraid of making mistakes), and they focus only on Japan and are less interested in interacting with non-Japanese. To survive and do well in the tight economic environment, some became so "efficiency-driven" that they don't even try to examine new or different ideas or try to cultivate relationships with others whom they perceive as "outsiders." Some have even told me that those attempts are "meaningless" or "irrelevant."

Meanwhile, the world has changed exponentially. The Internet has helped people, even in war zones, overcome

僭越ながら

　日本の皆さんにメッセージを送りたかったのですが、ごく個人的なものなので、章の中には含めませんでした。「おわりに」のかわりに、僭越ながら私の意見を書きたいと思います。

　二十年以上前に異文化トレーナー、コーチとして働き始めたとき、この仕事はいずれなくなるだろうと思いました。日本人は世界に出ていき、ネットワークを築き、より重要な世界の構成員になるだろうと思ったのです。実際、ビジネスやボランティア活動、日常生活の中で、世界で活躍の場を得て自分の知識や技術、見識を通じて素晴らしい貢献をされている多くの方に会いました。

　しかし、特に2008年の金融危機のあと、別の傾向が目につくようになりました。日本人の中に、極端なリスク回避（間違いを恐れる）に走る人が出てきて、彼らは、日本国内のことだけを考え、海外の人とのやりとりへの興味が薄れてしまいました。厳しい経済環境で、生き残り、成果を出すために、「効率第一」を標榜するあまり、新しいアイデアや違うアイデアを検討しようともせず、また「部外者」と思う人たちとは人間関係を築こうともしないのです。中には、そういう頑張り方（日本人以外の人と共に働くこと）は「意味がない」とか「自分とは関係ない」と私に言った人もいました。
　そうこうするうちに、世界はものすごいスピードで変わりました。インターネットのおかげで、人々——戦争地域に住む人たちで

geographical distances and time differences. With it, more people in the world have gotten over the language barrier. As a result, they have become a part of the constantly evolving world.

Back when I started working as an intercultural trainer and coach, I thought that only those who were in leadership roles (managers or otherwise) should acquire the courage, curiosity, and communication skills they needed to be part of the global field. But the times have changed. Now every person at every level and field needs to have those attributes or at least make an effort to have them. Otherwise, it takes too long to move large organizations. Think about this: if only one person out of five people understands a discussion in English, the discussion process becomes significantly slower. If four people out of five understand it, that can speed things up. Time has always been of the essence in work and life, but its speed is now accelerating across the world, and somehow we need to be in sync with it.

It seems to me that we are now losing ground because we don't have the right attitude to deal with this constantly changing world. Japan made a strategic move in 1639 to close its ports to foreign countries. Even Japanese who happened to be out of the country couldn't come back to Japan. It didn't seem to have occurred to the Tokugawa Shogunate that isolating Japan from the world in order to protect it from outside influences would have major consequences.

さえ——が地理的な距離や時差を乗り越えるようになりました。それとともに、世界中の多くの人たちが言語の壁を乗り越え、常に進化している世界へ飛び込んでいったのです。

　異文化トレーナー、コーチとして働き始めたころ、私は、リーダーシップを担っている人たち（管理職であるかどうかに関わりなく）だけが、グローバルな場面で活躍するための勇気と興味、コミュニケーション・スキルを身につければよいと考えていました。しかし、時代は変わったのです。現在は、どの分野のどのレベルの人も、そういった特性を身につける、もしくは、身につけようと努力することが必要です。そうでないと、大きな組織をタイミングよく動かすことができません。考えてみてください。もし、五人のうち一人だけが英語での議論を理解できたとしたら、議論を進めるのにものすごい時間がかかります。もし五人のうち四人が理解できれば、議論のスピードアップをはかれます。仕事でも生活の場でも、時間は常に大事な要素でしたが、時間の流れのスピードは世界中で加速しています。私たち日本人も、そのスピードについていかなければなりません。

　常に変わりつつある世界への対応に適した心の姿勢が備わっていないために、日本が世界での存在感を失いつつあるように思えます。日本は1639年に、外国船の来航禁止政策を実施しました。当時、たまたま海外にいた日本人も帰国することができませんでした。海外の影響から守るために日本を世界から隔離することが、国の将来に大きな影響をもたらすとは、徳川幕府には思いもよらなかったようです。幸いにも、1854年に米国海軍のマシュー・ペリー提督が徳川幕府に開港を余儀なくさせました。そ

Fortunately, in 1853, an American, Commodore Matthew Perry, forced the Tokugawa Shogunate to open the country. That's how the isolation era of over two hundred years ended.

In my view, we're now isolating ourselves from the world, not by a conscious strategy, but by psychological retreat. I truly hope that we'll regain our will and confidence to get back in the game. There won't be a Matthew Perry of our time to force us to fully engage with the world. It is totally up to us.

Stay positive and gain speed

To be in sync and increase the speed of advancements, and to play a greater role in the global field, we need to find ways to make better decisions on when and where to use our energy. One of the things we can do is to stretch ourselves mentally.

■Suggestions [1]
Eliminate inertia

We like doing things in set ways that have been proven to be best or right. There are two potential pitfalls with this. One, sometimes it becomes the only way, and we lose our flexibility. Two, we sometimes don't remember why we're doing something in a certain way or why we are doing it at all, but we still keep doing it. Possibly, we already know it's a lost cause, but we don't stop to re-examine it or are afraid of raising the issue. We need to encourage ourselves to take

うして、二百年以上にわたる鎖国が終わりました。

　今日本は、意識的な対外政策ではなく、心理的な引きこもりのせいで自分たちを世界から孤立させているように思います。日本人が世界の人と向き合う意志と自信を取り戻し、世界で活躍することを心から願っています。今の時代には、世界とがっぷり取り組むことを日本に迫る、マシュー・ペリーのような人は現れないでしょう。私たち自身が将来への鍵を握っているのです。

前向きな態度で、スピードを上げる

　歩調を合わせ前進するスピードを上げ、世界の場でより大きな役割を果たすには、私たちのエネルギーを投入するタイミングと場をより的確に判断しなければなりません。そのためにできることの一つは、私たちの考え方を広げることです。

■提案 [1]
慣性を排除する

　私たちは、ベストもしくは正しいとされる一定のやり方で物事を進めるのが好きです。これには、二つの落とし穴が潜んでいます。まず、そのやり方が唯一のやり方となってしまい、融通が利かなくなってしまうこと。そして二つ目は、時として、あることを特定のやり方でしている理由がわからなかったり、もともとそれをする理由もわからなかったりするのに、それでも同じことをやり続けてしまうことです。もうその作業に意味がないことを知りながら、立ち止まって再検討しなかったり、問題提起に消極的

a fresh look at whatever it may be. Inertia with a lost purpose results in a lot of lost time in our work and life.

■ Suggestions [2]

Increase the positives and worry less about the negatives

Think big and find ways to do things that benefit to many people. Encourage others to do what they want or lift many people's spirits, rather than making things even or equal to everyone. People are usually happier when they're gaining something like knowledge, skills, money, and the right level of challenges. Ask yourself, "What do I want?" and ask others, "What do you want?"

■ Suggestions [3]

Find a positive way of spending your energy when you find yourself criticizing others

We love it when something is beautifully done, whether it's artwork or dinner or sports. But we also tend to quickly criticize others' work when it's not well done. Or even when it's well done, we may doubt their motives and try to find ways to bring them down. When Nobukazu Kuriki failed his many attempts to reach the peak of Mount Everest, some were quick to criticize him. I wonder why we expect others to be perfect when we ourselves are not. What he tried to do was

になったりします。それが何であれ、新鮮な目で見直すことを自己奨励する必要があります。目的を失った慣性は、私たちの仕事と生活に大きな無駄を生みます。

■提案［2］
よい点を広め、不足を心配しすぎない

　大きく考え、多くの人に利益を行き渡らせる方法を考えましょう。物事を誰にとっても平等にするのではなく、人がしたいことをするのを応援し、多くの人を元気づけましょう。人はたいてい、知識や技術、お金、そして自分のレベルに合ったチャレンジを得ていると幸せに感じます。自分に向かって「私が希望するものは何か？」と自問し、人にも「あなたが希望するものは何ですか？」と聞いてみてください。

■提案［3］
人を非難している自分に気づいたら、エネルギーを前向きに使う方法を考える

　美術であれ夕食であれスポーツであれ、出来栄えが素晴らしいと大変うれしいものです。一方、しあがりがもう一つだと、私たちは人の仕事をすぐ非難しがちです。ときには、なかなかの出来であっても、その人の真意を疑ったり、その人の仕事の価値を下げようとしたりします。登山家の栗城史多がエベレスト登頂に何度も失敗すると、すぐに非難する人たちがいました。私たち自身が完璧ではないのに、どうして人に完璧さを求めるのか不思議です。彼が遂げようとしたことは、とてつもないチャレンジで、賞

a tremendous challenge, and admirable. He wanted to share that experience with people who may be struggling in their everyday life. I'm all for different views and opinions. We don't have to agree on everything that he did or tried to do, but there was something good and beautiful about him.

I'd like us all to be appreciative of someone's attempts to do something well, especially when he or she is doing it to inspire and encourage others by doing his or her best.

I hope we'll become more appreciative and supportive of those who take risks with good intentions, and try to learn from them. If we are inclined to criticize others, that will diminish us psychologically and we may decide to do only what we know we can do, because we don't want to be criticized by others. Criticizing others doesn't lead to anybody's happiness or hopeful future.

We can gain speed by being positive, and grow more if we support each other. A positive and supportive attitude may also increase our joy in life.

The following questions may help you shift your mindset in a positive direction:

- Was there something positive about my (friend's/ colleague's/other's) experience?
- What would be a good next step for me and the people involved?

賛に値します。彼は毎日の生活で苦労している人と、エベレスト登山の経験を共有したかったのです。いろんな見方や意見があることには大賛成です。彼がしたことや、しようとしたことすべてに同意する必要はありませんが、彼には立派で美しい何かがありました。

日本人には、人が何かをやり遂げようとする試みを好意的に評価する人たちであってほしいです。特に、その人が自分の最善を尽くすことで人をやる気にさせ、応援しようとしているときには、なおさらです。

価値ある何かを目指し、リスクを承知で物事に取り組む人たちを高く評価、応援し、彼らから学ぶ意欲を持ちたいものです。人の非難に走りがちだと、自分自身が精神的に縮こまってしまうだけでなく、人に非難されたくないので、できることしかしないようになってしまいます。人を非難しても、誰の幸せにも、希望のある未来にもつながりません。

前向きな態度で物事に取り組むとスピードを上げられますし、お互いを支援することで成長もできます。前向きでお互いを支え合う態度は、人生の喜びにもつながります。

以下の質問は、あなたの心を前向きに転換するのに役立つと思います。

- 私の（人の）経験の中に、評価できる何かがあったか？
- 私と周りの人がとるべき、次のステップは何か？

Be aware that people outside Japan have their own operating systems

I understand that being polite is paramount in Japan to keep things smooth and harmonious. But non-Japanese, especially in business, usually care much less about this. So, when you see things moving forward but find yourself emotionally left behind, it's probably a good idea to move forward along with others. Your emotional hang-up caused by others' behaviors (she didn't thank me or he didn't apologize for his mistake, or they didn't let me know when they received that important information) will cause you to engage less fully, and can cause a delay on what you're doing, and that could slow your group down.

An American astrophysicist, Neil deGrasse Tyson said, "The universe is under no obligation to make sense to you." The same can be said about cultural differences. One of my colleagues reminds others that Japanese have their own justifiable reasons to do things in certain ways, and so do people in other cultures. So, please try not to judge others (Japanese or not) immediately, and ask questions and try to understand why they want what they want, or why they do things in ways that are different from yours.

海外の人たちには彼らなりの思考・行動システムがある

　物事をつつがなく進め、和を保つために、日本では礼儀正しくあることが何よりも大切なのは承知しています。しかし海外の人たちは、とくに仕事では、丁寧であることにそれほど気を遣いません。ですから、物事が前に進んでいるにも関わらず、自分が感情的に取り残されていると感じたら、周りの人たちと一緒に前に向かって進むことを選んでください。他人の態度にわだかまりを感じていると（彼女は感謝してくれなかった、彼は間違ったのにあやまらなかった、重要な情報を受け取ったときにすぐ私に教えてくれなかった）、相手や仕事とがっぷり四つに組めませんし、自分の作業に遅れが生じ、その結果、あなたのグループの仕事にも余計な時間がかかってしまうかもしれません。

　アメリカ人の天体物理学者、ニール・デグラス・タイソンは、著書の中で「宇宙は、あなたに納得してもらえなくても一向にかまわない」と述べました。私の同僚の一人は、日本人には日本人なりのやり方を正当化できる理由があるのと同様に、他の文化の人たちにも自分たちのやり方を正当化できる理由がある、と念を押します。どうか、人（日本人であれ、海外の人であれ）のことをすぐに決めつけず、なぜその人が特定のものを欲しいのか、また、なぜ人があなたと違うやり方で物事を進めるのか、質問をして理解に努めてください。

Be courageous—think about opportunity costs

Japanese are, in general, past oriented. The past is real, as it is an accumulation of things that already happened (facts) and experiences. So, we tend to trust the past more than the future. However, in today's world where things are moving and changing fast, we need to think about opportunity costs. When we choose A and not B, then not pursuing B is an opportunity cost. It doesn't show up as a result, for we can't really measure the impact of not doing B.

Let's say an opportunity appeared in front of us. It's a bridge to the other side of a river. I can think of three scenarios that can result in invisible and immeasurable opportunity costs.

One, we may lose the opportunity to succeed because we don't make our decisions fast enough. Harmony within a group is paramount in Japan; however, if we prioritize harmony over everything else, our ability to move quickly suffers.

Two, the Japanese cultural brake, summarized in the proverb, *Ishibashi wo tataite wataru* stalls us on this side of the bridge. The direct translation of this proverb is, "Walk over the stone bridge after you make sure it's safe by tapping it." Viewed optimistically, such behavior can be a sign of prudence; however, this should also be recognized as a sign of risk avoidance that can cost us greatly. Today, some people say, "Japanese break the stone bridge by tapping it too hard."

度胸をつける——機会費用（見えない利益の損失）を考える

　日本人は一般に過去を中心に考えます。過去はすでに起こったこと（事実）と経験の積み重ねですから、現実です。ですから、未来よりも過去を信用しがちです。しかし、物事の進歩と変化が速い現在の世界では、機会費用について考える必要があります。BではなくAを選択すると、Bを選択しないことが、機会費用になります。Bを実行しない影響は測定できないので、その費用を結果として示すことはできません。

　私たちの目の前に、ある機会が現れたとしましょう。川の向こう側へ渡る橋です。目に見えず、測定もできない機会費用が生じる三つのシナリオが考えられます。

　まず、渡るか渡らないかの決定に時間がかかりすぎ、成功する機会を失ってしまうかもしれません。グループ内での和は日本では非常に大切ですが、和を何事にも優先すると、素早い行動力が発揮できません。

　二つ目は、「石橋を叩いて渡る」の諺に象徴される日本の文化的なブレーキが、橋のこちら側でもたもたする状況を作ります。この諺の直訳は、「石橋を叩いて安全であることを確かめてから、歩いて渡りなさい」です。好意的に見れば、これは思慮深さの表れです。しかし同時に、後に大きなツケを生じるリスク回避としても認識するべきです。現代は、「日本人は石橋を叩きすぎて壊す」という人もいます。すべてに間違いがないようにするのは、日本人の本能でもあり常識であると言ってもいいでしょう。しかし、

Making sure everything is in order is almost a Japanese instinct and common sense. But while we take too much time to go forward, we may lose the window of opportunity, and the stone bridge may disappear in front of our eyes before we cross it, or worse, while we're on it.

Three, we have decided to cross the bridge, and justified the decision by analyzing the risks. It has taken a long time to make a sound decision with many supporters, and luckily, the bridge is still there. But we are not moving forward because of our general fear about things that are new and different. "There have been no precedents" can be a valid reason in Japan for not trying something new and different. But how can we know for sure if this new thing or that different idea will or won't expand our opportunities in the future? We'll never know until we try.

The opportunity cost doesn't show up as a loss in the numbers, as we didn't see an actual result from our quick decision-making, risk-taking, and fearless action. But too much caution can possibly make us miss out on a path for a better result or even a better future. If this happens in life, the invisible cost could be a new relationship, a new endeavor, or personal growth. We know we can learn from our mistakes and failures. So, let's have the courage to choose action more often and not hold on to the past to stay where we are.

Most people learn from their experiences, both successes or failures. Even if we fail, we can learn from it and move forward.

もたもたしているうちにせっかくの好機を取り逃がし、渡る前に橋が目の前から消えてしまうかもしれませんし、悪くすると、橋を渡っている最中に消えてしまうかもしれません。

　三つ目のシナリオです。橋を渡ることにし、リスクを分析して、その決断の正当性を証明しました。時間をかけて、多くの支援者とともにしっかりした意思決定をし、幸運にも橋はまだあります。しかし、新しく今までとは違う物事に対する全般的な恐れから、前進することができません。日本では、「前例がない」は、新しいことや今までと違うことに取り組まない理由として認められています。しかし、新しいものや違ったアイデアが将来の私たちの機会を拡大するかしないかを、どうやって判断できるのでしょうか？やってみるまで、わからないのです。

　素早い意思決定、リスクの負担、大胆な行動が生む結果を現実に見ることができないので、機会費用は数字としては表れません。けれども、用心深すぎると、よりよい成果やよりよい将来への道／橋を逃してしまうかもしれません。これが人生で起こると、目に見えない費用は新しい人間関係、新しい挑戦、人としての成長などが考えられます。自分の間違いや失敗から学べることはわかっています。ですから、もっと行動を選ぶ勇気を持ち、現状確保のために過去にしがみつかないようにしましょう。

　多くの人は、経験——成功と失敗の両方——から学びます。失敗してもそこから学び、前に進むことができるのです。

Goals first

"Goals" here refer to what you and/or your group wants. In other words, the details of the situation or history (how you got here) isn't of much importance. I know Japanese want to confirm the situation over and over, as we believe by doing so, a solution can emerge. Unfortunately, this traditional and natural-for-Japanese approach usually takes a long time to find a solution or to find the next step that will get us closer to the solution. So, we need to learn how to live with "just enough" understanding of a situation.

One way to do this is to focus on what would be the desired outcome or situation we'd like to find ourselves in. To make this work, you and your group members need to agree on this approach, the solution-focused approach. Even for a strong leader, it's a constant challenge to lead a group of people who want to know every detail of a situation. To make our work easier and faster and effective, we need to cultivate a culture of goal-orientation or solution-focus. In short, we need to focus on the items that will bring better results.

If you want to be a leader

If you want to be a leader in a conventional sense, you need a follower or followers. You can lead others even if you're not a manager or someone with authority. I recommend that you

目標を第一に

ここでの「目標」は、あなたやあなたのグループが望むものです。つまり、細かい状況や今までの経過は、あまり重要ではありません。日本人は状況を確認する中で解決方法が見えてくると信じているので、状況を丁寧に何度も確認したがります。残念ながら、この伝統的で日本人にとっては当たり前のやり方では、解決方法や解決方法につながる次のステップの見極めに時間がかかります。ですから、「最低限十分な（完全ではなく）」状況の理解で済ませるようにしなければなりません。

そうするための一つの方法は、希望する結果や望ましい状況に焦点を当てることです。うまく実行するには、あなたのグループの人が、この解決中心のやり方に合意する必要があります。状況のすべての詳細を知りたい人たちを統率するのは、優れたリーダーにとっても息を抜けないチャレンジです。仕事をやりやすくし、早くかつ効果的にしあげるには、目標中心または解決中心の文化を作らなければなりません。要するに、よりよい結果につながるものに、エネルギーを集中するということです。

リーダーになりたければ

普通に考えれば、リーダーになりたければあなたに従う人が必要です。あなたが管理職でなくても、権限がなくても、人をリードすることができます。私が推薦するのは、前向きな行動でリー

lead by positive behaviors. If you're a person who tends to say, "Do as I say," or "Don't make mistakes," to others often, then you're probably not a leader yet, no matter where you are in your organization. I hope your positive behavior will inspire others to be positive, productive, and goal-oriented. Here's what John Quincy Adams, the sixth president of the United States, said about leadership:

"If your actions inspire others to dream more, learn more, do more and become more, you are a leader."

Lead yourself in self-development

Write down your own IMHO. It doesn't have to be about achievements. It can be about your attitude towards life (being positive or being kind, for example), or directions (trying to find new things that can be of your interest) or something that you want to explore (visiting castles in Europe and learning about their architecture).

Then, try to find a supporter of your IMHO. It's hard to keep going all by yourself. If you can find someone or a group of people who can encourage each other in their pursuit of their individual IMHO, that'd be wonderful. Flexibility is an important key here. It's rare to find a perfect supporter who

ドすることです。もしあなたが、人に「私の言った通りにしなさい」「間違わないように」と頻繁に言う人であれば、組織内での職位に関係なく、おそらくあなたはまだリーダーにはなれていません。あなたの前向きな行動が、周りの人を触発し、前向きであろうと思わせ、よりよい成果への意欲を湧かせ、また目標から目をそらさない態度を身につけさせます。以下は、アメリカの第六代大統領のジョン・クウィンシー・アダムズが、リーダーについて述べたものです。

「もしあなたの行動が、人に勇気やヒントを与え、彼らがもっと夢を膨らませ、もっと学び、もっと実行し、人として成長すれば、あなたはリーダーです」

自分をリードして、自己開発をする

ご自分の「僭越ながら」を書いてみてください。達成したい目標以外のことでもよいのです。あなたの人生に対する態度（前向きであること、親切であることなど）や方向性（興味を持てそうな新しいことを探してみる）、または探求したいこと（ヨーロッパの城を訪れて、城の建築について学ぶ）でもいいのです。

そして、あなたの「僭越ながら」を支援してくれる人を見つけます。自分一人で頑張り続けるのは難しいものです。お互いに自分の「僭越ながら」に近づこうとするのを励まし合える人や、グループを見つけられると、最高です。柔軟であることも、大事です。あなたのことを完璧に理解してくれる支援者を見つけること

understands you perfectly. In fact, if she or he has different views, that'd be better. You can examine yourself deeper and wider, and can come up with a better idea or greater confidence. Please also review your IMHO and update it as you go along.

I'd like to share a poem written by Beah Richards (1920–2000), an African American actress and poet. This poem is my IMHO expressed much more beautifully than I could ever say it myself. I have this poem on the wall in my home office. Whenever I could use a push from someone else, I read this and then start the day fresh.

Today
by Beah Richards

Today is ours, let's live it
And love is strong, let's give it
A song can help, let's sing it
And peace is dear, let's bring it
The past is gone, don't rue it
Our work is here, let's do it
Our world is wrong, let's right it
The battle hard, let's fight it
The road is rough, let's clear it
The future vast, don't fear it

は、なかなかありません。むしろ、相手が別の見方を持っていたら、その方がよいのです。あなた自身を深くまた広く見つめることで、よりよいアイデアが出てきたり、より大きな自信を抱くことになるでしょう。また、ご自分の「僭越ながら」を時おり再検討し、更新してください。

　ここに、アフリカ系アメリカ人の女優で詩人、ビア・リチャーズ（1920–2000）の書いた詩を紹介します。この詩は私の「僭越ながら」を、私には到底真似できない美しさで表現しています。この詩を、ホーム・オフィスの壁に貼っています。誰かに励ましてもらいたいとき、この詩を読んで、仕切り直します。

　　今日
　　ビア・リチャーズ

　　今日は私たちのもの　生きよう
　　愛は力強い　分け与えよう
　　歌が助けてくれる　歌おう
　　平和が愛しい　連れてこよう
　　過去は昔のこと　嘆くのをやめよう
　　私たちの仕事はここにある　取り組もう
　　世界が間違っている　正そう
　　戦いは苦しい　立ち向かおう
　　道は険しい　切り開こう
　　未来は果てしなく広がる　恐れずに進もう

Is faith asleep? Let's wake it
Today is ours, let's take it

With hope for a bright future,
Michiko Schwab

信心が眠っている？ 叩き起こそう
今日は私たちのもの　我がものにしよう

明るい未来を願って
しゅわぶ美智子

English **C**onversational **A**bility **T**est
国際英語会話能力検定

● E-CATとは…
英語が話せるようになるための
テストです。インターネット
ベースで、30分であなたの発
話力をチェックします。

www.ecatexam.com

● iTEP®とは…
世界各国の企業、政府機関、アメリカの大学
300校以上が、英語能力判定テストとして採用。
オンラインによる90分のテストで文法、リー
ディング、リスニング、ライティング、スピー
キングの5技能をスコア化。iTEP®は、留学、就
職、海外赴任などに必要な、世界に通用する英
語力を総合的に評価する画期的なテストです。

www.itepexamjapan.com

心が伝わる英語の話し方

2020年1月9日　第1刷発行

著　者　　しゅわぶ美智子

発行者　　浦 晋亮

発行所　　IBC パブリッシング株式会社
　　　　　〒162-0804 東京都新宿区中里町29番3号 菱秀神楽坂ビル9F
　　　　　Tel. 03-3513-4511 Fax. 03-3513-4512
　　　　　www.ibcpub.co.jp

印刷所　　新灯印刷株式会社

ISBN978-4-7946-0613-6